The Pow Pussy

Part Two

by

Kara King

Copyright 2013

1-1045742611

© Kara King

All Rights Reserved

No part of this book may be reproduced in any form or by any electronic or mechanical means including information storage and retrieval systems, without permission in writing from the author. For information about special discounts for bulk purchases or for all other business matters, please contact youwantthep@gmail.com.

DISCLAIMER AND/OR LEGAL NOTICES

The information presented herein represents the view of the author as of the date of publication. Due to the rate at which conditions change, the author reserves the right to alter and update her opinion based on new conditions.

This material is general dating advice only and is not intended to be a substitute for professional medical or psychological advice. This book is for entertainment purposes only. This book contains sexually explicit material and is not intended for persons under the age of eighteen (18).

TABLE OF CONTENTS

Introduction 7
PART ONE: MORE POWER! 11
Chapter One: The Power of the Personality 12
    Personality Traits That Men Adore 13
    Drawing Men to You Naturally 16
    The Smile Trick 17
    You're Too Sexy 19
    The Good and the Bad Side of Being Outgoing 20
    Places to Meet Men 22
Chapter Two: The Power of Staying Single 25
    Getting to Know Yourself 27
    My Personal Catalyst to Self-Discovery 29
    Look at it From the Other Way Around 31
    Enjoying Freedom 32
    Overcoming Fear 34
    Doing Things for Yourself 35
    Commitment Being Your Choice 36
Chapter Three: The Power of Being a Woman of Integrity 39
    Pussy Power Devaluation 41
    Karma is a Cunt 43
    Camaraderie Between Women 43
    Why? 44
    The Ego High 45
    But, I Love Him 46
    The Test 47

Don't Learn the Hard Way 48
An Open Letter to the Mistresses 49
A Man of Integrity 50

Chapter Four: The Power of Choosing Your Battles 53
The Nagger 57
The Push Over 59
The Fighter 62
The Perfectionist 70
Why Are We So Damn Picky? 73
Choosing Wisely 74
Admitting When You're Wrong 75

Chapter Five: The Power of Food, Sex, and Loyalty 77
How To Keep a Good Man by Your Side for Life 78
When Food, Sex, and Loyalty Doesn't Work 80
FOOD 81
SEX 83
LOYALTY 90

Chapter Six: The Power of the Married Pussy 94
Teaching an Old Dog New Tricks 95
The Five "P's" 96
Why Your Power May Have Been Disconnected 101
Patience and Persistence 101
What to do if You Encounter Resistance 102
Positive Reinforcement 103
Pussy Negotiations 105
Going to War 106
What if He Cheats? 109
Should I Take Him Back? 112

Chapter Seven: The Power of the Divorced Pussy 114
    Positive Perspective.. 117
    The Five Steps of Positive Perspective 117
    When All Else Fails.. 126
    The Husband and the Whore 127
    The Upgrade 129
    Children and Divorce 131

PART TWO: MAN POWERS.. 135

Chapter Eight: The Power of the Baby Daddy 136
    The Dream.. 137
    Financial Power... 139
    The Kids 140
    Should I Stay or Should I Go? 141
    The Seven Questions 142
    Abuse is More Than a Slap in the Face 147
    Financial Abuse 147
    Sexual Abuse 148
    Verbal, Mental, and Emotional Abuse..................... 149
    What to Do If You Have Nowhere to Turn 151
    Pros and Cons.. 152
    Your Answer.. 153

Chapter Nine: The Power of Mr. Good Dick 156
    Using Mr. Good Dick 158
    The Curious Case of Mr. Good Dick....................... 158
    Dick Decisions 162
    Don't Slip... 164

Chapter Ten: The Power of Rejection 166
    Why is Rejection so Powerful? 167

    How Does Rejection Affect Us?..168
    How to Overcome Rejection 169
Chapter Eleven: The Power of the Patriarchy....................172
    Dude, Where's My Pussy Power?...175
    Patriarchy:...178
    Bullshit, Hypocrisy, and Mind Games..................................178
    The Evil Side of Patriarchy 181
    Conditioning AKA MANipulation 187
    Woman's Work...190
    How Patriarchy Affects Men 192
    Nice Guys Shouldn't Finish Last 192
Conclusion 196
Frequently Asked Questions 200
Song List..215

Introduction

I wrote "The Power of the Pussy" with the sole intention of letting women know that we have the power, and therefore we don't need to take crap from any man, for any reason. Honestly, I had no other agenda other than empowering women. Little did I know that I was stirring up controversy with every page. I really pissed some people off! It was fun.

Since then I've been called a feminist. I've been called a misogynist. I've even been called a man hater from hell. But, what I've never been called is a doormat, fool, or push over. Call me what you want, but the powers laid out in the first book have worked magic in my life and the lives of women all over the world. I've received thousands of emails from women stating that the powers have changed their lives for the better.

Since implementing the powers in my own life, I've never had a broken heart, been cheated on, dumped, or played for a fool. I've been happily married for twelve years to an amazing gentleman that treats me like a queen. So, call me what you want, but I know what works with men and what doesn't. I'm not about to keep this information a secret. I'm going to share it with women everywhere. Sorry guys, but the cat's out of the bag...

The first book, "The Power of the Pussy," empowered women by changing the way they think about men and dating. In that book, I laid down the foundation of pussy power. Part two is going to provide you with tips, tricks, and advice that will build upon the knowledge in the first book. So, if you haven't already, I highly suggest you read the first book.

This follow up book, "The Power of the Pussy: Part Two," is going to go into more detail and cover a broad range of situations. These situations include divorce, marriage, the single life, dealing with baby daddy drama, infidelity, and a variety of other common situations. It's my hope that both books will be used as guides to help women navigate through the complexities of womanhood. It's my goal that they will both serve as motivation and encouragement through the trials and tribulations that we all may come across at some point in our lives.

This follow up book is a little bit different than the first book, as it's broken down into two sections. Section one will discuss more of the powers that we have as women. If you have your journal or completed assignments from book one, keep them handy. This book will continue in the spirit of the first book by asking you questions and provoking thought about your unique situation.

Section two will discuss powers that men have over us. Being aware of the grip that men can potentially have over us is empowering in itself. That's because their powers can distract us from using our own powers. They have the ultimate ability to make us powerless, therefore it's imperative that we're aware of these magical penis powers.

And of course, just like the first book, I need to warn you that I will be very blunt. I don't want to waste anyone's time by beating around the bush. For those new to my writing, please know that I use curse words, and I speak about controversial topics that could be considered "politically incorrect".

Women need this empowerment now more than ever because a lot of us have been too nice, too naive, or too passive and it's gotten us into bad situations. There's nothing wrong with being nice, but some men have learned how to take this kindness for weakness. Unfortunately, that's led to some of us experiencing heartache, lies, games, and cheating, time and time again.

It's time for that nonsense to stop. It's time to give the bad guys a taste of their own medicine. It's time to flip the game around on them, and it's also time we decide to only give our love and respect to the good men of this world.

The problem we face as women is that when we try to have a little fun and play games, or do the same things men do, we're shamed and made to feel wrong. Meanwhile, they can run around doing whatever they like and no one even blinks an eye. This is no accident. We've been conditioned by society to act and behave in ways that benefit males, simply because society is run by men.

Ladies, they've tricked us! Tricked us into thinking it's okay to rush into sex, then they turn around and shame us when we do it. They've tricked us into feeling guilty for doing the same things that they do. But, worst of all, they've tricked us into settling for less than what we deserve. Well, the fun and games are over boys. It's time for us to do what makes us happy, do it without guilt, and stop worrying about what society thinks. It's our turn for a little bit of fun.

You know it's funny, there are some men out there that are all mad about these books, calling them "sexist." However, when you ask these same men, "Would you not want your daughter or sister to know this information?" They all say yes. So, when it comes to the women they date, or women in general, the advice is bad. But, when it comes to the women they love, the advice is on the money.

That alone speaks volumes about the content of these books. It's because pussy power is an invaluable characteristic that all women have, but men only want the women they love knowing this stuff. They don't want every woman knowing, because when used properly it enables women to automatically detect when a man's playing games.

When this power is cultivated and used in your daily life you will become unstoppable. You will be able to handle situations with fierce feminine wisdom. You will be able to hold your own in any situation, whether that's going out and conquering the male dominated world, getting your husband to feel the way he did 20 years ago, or simply getting a man's attention set on you.

Every woman possesses this power. That's the amazing thing about it. It doesn't matter who you are or what you've been through. It doesn't matter your age, what you look like, or what size you are. The only thing that hinders you is being unaware of this power. Being aware of it is half the battle; the other half is practicing it and using it in your everyday life. When you do, pussy power will leave you feeling empowered and ready to handle anything a man throws your way!

Part One:
More Power!

Part one of the book is the first seven chapters. Each chapter is going to introduce a new power. Some powers will be more for single women, and others will be more for committed women. However, all of these chapters will cover issues and topics that all of us may come to deal with, or have dealt with, at some point in our lives.

Chapter One

The Power of the Personality

Forget about a pretty face and a nice body. Ask any man and he will tell you that without a good personality, none of that superficial stuff matters. As I mentioned briefly in the first book, great looks will have men desiring you, but it won't have them getting down on one knee and eager to dedicate their lives to you. That's why it's imperative that we never under-estimate the power of the personality.

The power of the personality is why you see men head over heels in love with average-looking women. It's the same reason why we can get totally hung up on an average-looking guy. Personality is important for obvious reasons. No one wants to be with a boring person, a rude person, a conceited person, or a person with a self-centered personality. But, there's more to it than that.

The power of your unique personality is what will help you throughout the different phases of your love life. It's what will help you meet men when you're single. It will have them intrigued while you're dating. And it's what will make that special man fall in love with you, stay in love with you, and dedicate his life to you.

This chapter is not about changing who you are for a man. It's not about eliminating parts of your personality. It's simply going to be a section filled with bits and pieces of advice that you can sprinkle on top of your personality to help you bring out your inner vixen. Throughout this chapter I'm going to cover tips for women; such as finding the best places to meet men, tips for meeting men offline, and tactics to draw them in naturally. So, this chapter is going to cover a lot of things. All which relate in one way or another to the single most important and special part of a woman: her personality.

Personality Traits That Men Adore

I wanted to discover the personality traits that turned men

on the most. So, I did a lot of book research. In addition to this book research, I asked a group of single men to list their top five personality traits in a woman. After two of the ten men answered with descriptions of breasts, I reminded them that breasts were not personality traits. After this reminder, the men came up with fifty answers total. The five responses below were the answers that showed up *most frequently* from the men questioned and in the book research I found.

Chances are high that you have some of these personality traits within you. Know that whichever ones you have are valued deeply by men. Just like when we meet men with character, or men with great personality traits, we get turned on and impressed. Men like and appreciate this stuff too.

It's not all about butts and breasts. A thousand pretty girls with perfect bodies can come and go, but it's a woman's personality that makes a man fall in love. Personality, just like confidence, is a non-physical trait that's just as sexy, if not more, than physical appearance. Women with good personalities leave a lasting impression on men. Here are the top five personality traits out of fifty responses:

Intelligence – A lot of men appreciate an intelligent woman. Intelligence turns men on. It stimulates their interest. But, this is not about going to Harvard or becoming an intellectual. You don't have to be a genius to be labeled intelligent.

Intelligence comes in many forms. There's more than one way of being smart. Intelligence can be expressed in a multitude of ways, including (but not limited to) creativity, ambition, education, entrepreneurship, determination, accomplishments, and/or talents. Simply having goals and actively working towards them is sexy. Don't be ashamed of your nerdy side, your unique talents, or your interests. Be proud of your brain and never under-estimate the value it brings to your unique personality.

Sense of Humor – Ladies, you know how most of us love and appreciate a man that can make us laugh? It turns out that men love this quality just as much as we do. In turn, they also like when a woman appreciates their unique sense of humor. They enjoy when a woman can kick back, have a good time, and relax enough to be herself and let her sense of humor shine. If you're known to crack your friends up, but around men you feel too uncomfortable to let this side of yourself show, you need to work on your confidence.

Relax and let loose. Be your kooky, funny, or outrageous self. Don't ever worry about what a man's going to think. He's either going to "get you" or he won't. If he doesn't get your unique brand of humor, then you don't want to waste your time dating him anyways because he will probably end up boring you. If he does "get you" then he will admire your unique brand of funny and get turned on by it. Everyone loves to laugh, and if you can make a man laugh, that speaks volumes about your unique personality.

Kindness – Men love bitches, I agree. But they don't like rude bitches. In today's self-centered, self-serving world men have come to appreciate a woman who possesses some very simple, old-fashioned traits: Niceness. Consideration. Politeness. Kindness. Care and consideration for others. People have become so rude these days that finding a person who is kind has become a valued trait. Never disguise your politeness or mask it. If you're a sweetheart, let your kindness show. Just don't allow men to take your kindness for weakness.

Honesty and Faithfulness – Men apparently appreciate honesty and faithfulness just as much as we do. Just realize if you're an honest and faithful woman that these personality traits are appreciated by men. If you find that men are taking advantage of this part of your personality, you need to be more careful about who you're being faithful to. Look for men of integrity, men that value your honesty and faithfulness, not men that take advantage of it. For more details about this trait that men love, see the section titled, "Loyalty," under the chapter called The Power of Food, Sex, and Loyalty.

Appreciation – This was covered in book one, but seeing it repeated over and over again by the men only confirms its importance. Men like a pat on the back. Men NEED to feel appreciated, especially when they're good men and doing the right thing.

Just like we need to be told that we're beautiful, and we have a need to feel cherished by the man we love, they have a need to feel appreciated. It's all about boosting confidence for the other person. It feels good to get your ego stroked. We like it, and so do they. Hey, if you've got a good man, there's nothing wrong with boosting his confidence.

Appreciate the little things. Appreciate the big things. You should even appreciate the things you expect. This isn't about kissing a man's ass or constantly running behind him and thanking him for every little thing. Appreciation is about acknowledging when he's doing the right thing. It's about letting him know what you like about him. When his efforts are acknowledged and appreciated he will be eager to repeat that behavior over and over again. He will also appreciate that his woman has an appreciative personality.

Drawing Men to You Naturally

A lot of women desire to meet men in person. They prefer to avoid the online dating scene. There's nothing wrong with that. However, it should be understood that if you're not willing to smile and be friendly you're going to have a difficult time. To be successful at meeting men in public you have to send out a non-verbal message that says you're willing to engage. A signal that says, "I'm approachable. I'm single. Don't be afraid to come up and talk to me." Below I'm going to show you how to send out this non-verbal vibe and teach you how to draw men to you naturally.

First things first, if you walk around with a very serious face, you might have a problem meeting men in public. Some of us look bitchy or mad, even when we're not. I have that problem. My nose is turned up, and people automatically assume I'm a snob or a bitch, when in fact I'm the exact opposite. If people have told you before that you look mad, snobby, bitchy, angry, etc., then you have to put in a tiny bit of extra effort. You will have to intentionally look approachable or you'll look too intimidating for most men to get the courage to come up and talk to you.

Put on a small smile. You don't need to look crazy, walking around looking like the joker. Just crack a small smile. Look at yourself in the mirror. Take note of your normal facial stance. Then notice how you look with a smile. Can you make yourself appear friendlier with a small smile, without looking ridiculous?

The Smile Trick

When you're walking around out in public, don't stare at the floor. Walk with your head up high. This demonstrates confidence and approachability, but more importantly this allows you to do the smile trick.

The smile trick is for when you're out in public and you notice a cute guy or you catch a guy checking you out. If you like him, then don't be afraid to let him see you checking him out too. Let him notice you, noticing him. If he looks again, this is your chance to give him a little bit of a flirty smile.

Your smile will give him the okay to approach you if he's interested. If he's not a complete pussy, it will also give him the confidence to approach you and spark up a conversation. If he doesn't come up to you, then let it be. He was either just looking, he's in a relationship, or perhaps he's just too shy.

One of the most important things to know about meeting men out and about is that some men are afraid to approach us. You may have wondered in the past why men don't approach you. You think you're a pretty lady. What's the deal?

Honestly, some of them are terrified. *Especially the good ones*. So, that means sometimes YOU have to be more willing to be the outgoing one. If a man makes eye contact or is checking you out, don't look away. Smile pretty. Remember: it's okay to flirt, just do not pursue.

In the first book I talked about flirting without pursuing. When it comes to meeting men in public, you can bend this rule a little bit. You can be the first one to spark up conversation, the first to smile, or the first to flirt. You can get away with some pursuing because there's a big difference between flirting with men you know and flirting with random men in public. Allow me to explain...

The men you meet in public are going to be a lot more intimidated because they haven't had the time to gain the confidence and courage to approach you. They haven't had the time to figure out if you're single, or if you're even interested. Men don't like rejection, just like we don't like it. Rejection sucks. Unfortunately for them, they're the pursuers and this means they've got to get over the fear of rejection and just go for it. This requires a lot of self-coaching to gain the courage needed to pursue. Approaching women in public robs them of the time they need to gain that courage.

On the other hand, when you know a man through work, school, or some other day to day setting, he has had time to figure that stuff out. That's why there's no need for you to pursue. Obviously, when meeting men in public, these guys don't have that privilege and it makes a lot of them intimidated, scared, and confused. Especially if you're a really pretty woman. That's why we need to give them a boost when meeting men in public. Smiling, engaging, and being friendly and outgoing will give them the boost and approval they need to do their part and approach you.

A side note to the men reading this book, spying on our girl talk: The nice guys of this world have got to stop being so shy and scared of us. We want you to approach us. The approach is the man's job. If you want to meet women, you've got to get out there and be the aggressor.

Please, if you're a single, good-quality man... approach us. Flirt with us. We want good guys, but unfortunately a lot of the men that have the courage to approach us are the players. We can't tell the difference right away, so we have to go with the flow and work with whoever comes our way. Unfortunately for the good men of the world, this hurts your opportunities with women and it denies us the chance of meeting you.

Unfortunately, for women and the nice guys, it's usually the players and the douche bags that have the courage to come up to random women and spark up a conversation. It's only because they're very confident and comfortable talking to women. They've gotten over the fear of rejection. That's why "the asshole always gets the girl." The asshole isn't afraid to do his job as a man, and approach women.

It's because they're the ones willing to put themselves out there that Mr. Shy Nice Guy who is scared of rejection will never get anywhere. That's why I feel it's important to flash a smile. Let Mr. Shy Nice Guy know you're approachable and interested. Wipe away any fear of rejection a man may have by looking inviting and friendly. Besides, everyone looks prettier with a smile.

You're Too Sexy

It's important to look approachable when trying to meet men in public. However, sometimes our definition of what it means to look approachable can sabotage our efforts. This happens when we dress overly sexy. Looking too sexy in the wrong places, such as the grocery store or the gym, sends two bad messages.

Some guys may judge you by assuming that you're desperate or too eager for a man. While others may be too intimidated to talk to you.

Of course, if you're single you want to look good when you go out in public. I'm not saying to look like a slob. But, have you ever noticed that when you're wearing sweatpants, no makeup, and a frumpy bun—that's when men want to talk to you? That's because they feel less intimidated.

Begin to take notice of how you look when men approach you the most. It's usually a fine balance of looking cute, but not overly sexy. Which is ironic, because what other time would we be dolled up looking sexy, other than when we're single? Hello. Men. We're advertising. Duh.

A few other reasons why it's important not to look overly sexy everywhere you go, is because you want a man to like you for you. You also want to hold on to the opportunity of giving him something to look forward to, something to anticipate. If you're looking your best when he meets you, you lose out on your chance to wow him on that first date. He will have nothing to look forward to. You've used up your best tricks upon meeting him.

So, being too sexy hurts us in a few ways; it can send a message of desperation, it can intimidate men, and it can rob you of finding a man that thinks you're beautiful just the way you are. Besides, if he liked your normal, everyday look, imagine how it's going to turn him on to see you at your best on your first date.

The Good and the Bad Side of Being Outgoing

Meeting men in public and being able to naturally draw them to you requires some degree of being outgoing. For the shy girls this can make meeting men in public a difficult task. Whereas, if you're the more outgoing type, you may not have a problem with sparking up conversations with strangers or meeting men in public.

That's great news for you, because a lot of women have a hard time meeting guys while out and about. Being outgoing is a great trait to have when you're single.

BUT, there's a good and a bad side to everything. Be careful that you're not being too flirtatious, or you may be sending a bad message. Some men like to make assumptions and automatically conclude that if you're flirting with him, well then... you must want to suck his dick! Ummm... no asshole, we're just being flirty. Then there's the other end of the spectrum: the men that completely get caught off guard and don't know how to handle the flirty situation.

Use a fine balance of being friendly and flirty. And, if you're shy, step it up a notch. If you're naturally outgoing then just make sure you're not being *too* flirty when first meeting men in public. More intense flirting can be saved for second and third encounters, if they arise. Be outgoing and allow your personality to shine. Just be aware of yourself and pull back with the flirting if you think your "friendliness" is scaring men off or giving them the wrong impression.

Don't let this chapter intimidate you or turn you off from meeting men in public. **Remember, we have the upper hand.** Men are silly for titties. They're coo-coo for poo-tang. They can't help it. We have to spoon feed them the pussy or they get cocky and make assumptions. Or, the exact opposite happens: they get scared and confused. Ignore their testosterone-induced foolishness and simply have fun with them.

When you master the power of the personality, you will encounter endless opportunities to meet men in public. Mix that personality power with the power of confidence and top it all off with the power of the pussy and a lot of men will become putty in your hands. Don't take this whole meeting men in public thing too seriously. Always remember these last four things when implementing the advice in this chapter.

1) Men come a dime a dozen. If one guy doesn't respond or approach you, there's a thousand more coming right behind him.

2) Be confident. The power of confidence should never be under-estimated. It's very, very important.

3) Practice makes perfect. The more you implement the advice above, the more comfortable you will become with interacting with men in public. Of course, if you're new to all of this or you're shy, it's going to feel very strange at first. However, with time and practice any woman can become a master at drawing men to her.

4) Most importantly, have fun! When you're single the world is your candy store, and men are your candy. This is about YOU, not THEM. This isn't about throwing yourself out to the wolves like a piece of meat. It's about you getting out there and having a good time. It's about you enjoying the thrill of the hunt. Give a man a look, flash a pretty smile, and utilize the power of the pussy. Flirt. You're in the driver's seat. You're the seducer. Don't be scared to get out there and be a vixen.

Enjoy being single; you're free to do what you want, meet who you want, and be who you want. Embrace this time in your life by having fun with all of this. Dating and being single is not meant to be stressful. *If it ever gets too stressful, you're taking it too seriously. Relax and have fun.*

Places to Meet Men

If you want to get men to approach you, you've got to go where the men like to hang out. Below is a list of places where you can meet men, along with a few helpful hints.

Horse races on game day

The gym

Grocery store

Classes
(College, Trade school, cooking classes, etc...)

Coffee shop

Airport lounge
(If you travel a lot)

The beach

Gas station:
Pumping Gas / Putting air in your tires
(Hey, it worked for me!)

Church

Speed Dating

Local bar or restaurant near the arena after a big game or concert

Sports bars during a big game

Casinos
(Especially at the tables)

Bars near upscale work places
(Such as doctors', stock brokers', bankers', and lawyers' offices.)

Dog Park

Clubs that are hosting after parties for concerts

Music store
(Ex. Guitar Center)

Hardware store

The TV department/ hardware department of your local big box store

(These last three are great places because you can spark up a conversation by asking a question.)

Where you decide to go depends on what kind of man you're looking for. For example, if you're looking for an older, more mature man, you may want to go to the horse races when they're hosting a live race. If you love sports buffs, then go to the local pub on game night. If musicians turn you on, then go to live shows hosting local bands or music stores.

One thing that works (and this is going to sound crazy) is to go to a gas station, dressed somewhat nicely and put air in your tires or check your oil. Look around confused. I've noticed that men feel more comfortable approaching a woman when he sees a "damsel in distress." Also, you're in a man's element, so he feels he can offer you advice and help. Thus, giving him a boost in confidence.

Meeting men is a numbers game. The more men you interact and engage with, the higher the chances are that you will find the ones who are single and attracted to you. However, if you sit on the side lines, quietly waiting and hoping for men to come up and talk to you, you will die a lonely, old lady. That's why I always recommend online dating. It gives everyone the boost they need to interact freely. However, knowing how to draw men to you naturally is a personality power that every woman who's single should practice and master.

Chapter Two

The Power of Staying Single

"Being single used to mean that nobody wanted you. Now it means you're sexy, smart, and you're taking your time deciding how you want your life to be and who you want to spend it with."

There's a lot of power in being single *by choice*. I spoke about this briefly in the first book, but I want to dig deeper and go over exactly why staying single by choice empowers women. This advice is particularly useful to young women, who should enjoy their youth and try to remain single for as long as possible. However, every single woman, regardless of her age, should only remain single until she meets a man that's so amazing, she would be a fool to pass him up. Stay uncommitted until you meet a man that's your personal definition of a real man. (The guy that meets a majority of the attributes on your dream man list from book one.)

Until you find that man, you're single and loving it.

Don't be afraid to let people know that you're single. It's nothing to be ashamed of. Say it with pride. Let them know it's a personal decision. It's a <u>conscious choice</u> you've made because you want to enjoy your freedom and you're not willing to settle for anything less than the best. You can enjoy flings and short commitments, but don't settle down into a long term commitment until you've had several years on your own.

There are several reasons why this is very important and I will cover each reason below....

#1) Getting to Know Yourself

#2) Enjoying Freedom

#3) Over-Coming Fear

#4) A Time to Spoil Yourself

#5) Commitment is Your Choice

Getting to Know Yourself

The power of staying single enables you to truly embrace who you are as an individual. This is the journey of self-discovery that every woman needs to make at the beginning of her young life. However, if you're an older woman, and you missed this opportunity in your younger years, it's never too late to make this journey (if you haven't done so already). Getting to know yourself is important because it enables you to learn how to enjoy yourself, by yourself. I'm not talking about masturbation here. I'm talking about getting to know who you are, alone, without the influence of anyone but yourself.

You should take this time to discover who you are, who you want to be, what you want to accomplish in life, and the type of people you want to be around. Figure out what you like and what you don't like, independently from the opinions of others. This journey of getting to know yourself and discovering your personal identity is different than just developing confidence. It's actually the foundation or stepping stones to confidence. It's when you learn to love all that you've discovered, despite what other people think, that the power of confidence is able to come into your life and empower you even further.

So, you can love yourself and still lack confidence. Self-love and self-confidence are two separate traits. It's when these two elements are combined that a fierce woman emerges. A woman that can't be played. A woman that can't be broken. A woman that won't be changed simply to please a man. A woman that won't settle for less than the best.

Getting to know yourself, and then falling in love with all that you discover is very important when it comes to love. That's because you need to know who you are fully and truly, before entering into a relationship. Use this time to cultivate a relationship with yourself. Learn who you are and then...**fall in love with who you are.**

Once you've done this, you won't change yourself to please a man. You won't be faking who you are in order to obtain love and attention from a guy. You won't be easily influenced by guys. You will stand firm and not allow men (or anyone) to take advantage of you.

We've all heard the saying, "You must love yourself before others can love you." But, what does that really mean? Why must we love ourselves first? Someone can certainly love you if you don't love yourself. However, to have a *healthy* love, a *true* love, a *passionate* love, and a *lasting* love; one must learn to love themselves first and foremost.

The reason why self-love is healthy for your relationships is because you have to have a level of self-importance or you'll let people treat you badly. Even worse, you might not even realize that you're being treated badly. If you don't love yourself, you may be satisfied with very little. Just having a guy around paying attention to you would be enough to satisfy you. Simply having any relationship, even if it's an unhealthy one, would be enough to keep you happy.

Unfortunately, this ends up happening to a lot of women and it's a huge reason why they put up with cheaters, users, losers, and assholes. They've not learned to love themselves first and foremost. A woman that has taken the time to learn to love herself will not tolerate disrespect.

My Personal Catalyst to Self-Discovery

When I was nineteen years old I learned why it was so important to get to know myself. I was in a committed relationship with my high school sweetheart, who was my first long-term boyfriend. We'd been together for over four years when one day I came to the realization that he didn't know who I really was. I'd been putting parts of myself away from him and everyone around me. I was embarrassed of a simple, yet vital part of who I was: I loved rock music.

I was hiding my passion for rock music because I went to an inner-city school, where rock music was not in any way cool, let alone acceptable. But, it was my own insecurity, not my environment, that was the culprit. So, throughout my entire relationship, I kept this part of myself hidden. Until the day my boyfriend walked in and caught me off guard while I was blasting The Doors. He turned it off and said, "What the hell is this shit?" Then he put on some rap music.

I got so mad, but my anger had nothing to do with my boyfriend, my peers at school, or the music. My anger was with myself. That single moment had a huge impact on me because in that moment I realized I had created a problem for myself by not being myself. My anger had everything to do with the fact that I was suppressing who I was. I didn't have the courage to like what I liked. You see, I was so young that I hadn't taken the time to truly discover who I was. More importantly, I hadn't taken the time to be **proud** of who I was.

I eventually came to realize that I needed to take time to myself, to really discover who I was. To be free. As I mentioned in the first book, it was after that break up that I went on a journey of self-discovery. I told myself that I was going to be single and enjoy it. I was going to get to know myself and love myself, by myself.

This was when I felt like I truly blossomed. I found out

who Kara was. I became myself, separate from a man, separate from my parents, separate from any outsiders. This personal journey of self-discovery had a huge impact on me. My life changed for the better. That's why I feel so strongly that every woman needs to find the opportunity to go on this journey (if she hasn't done so already).

It's vital that we all get to know who we truly are and then become confident and proud of that person. When we have that self-acceptance we will not allow people (especially men) to influence us. We will have the pleasure and privilege of being comfortable in our own skin, comfortable within our relationships, and comfortable around others. We will not make sacrifices for others or tolerate bad treatment. The personal journey of self-discovery is a journey that every woman should make at some point in her life. Especially when she's in her younger years, or later in life, if she hasn't been able to previously do so.

I think every person goes through this to some extent as we grow older. Unfortunately, some of us go through it later in life or never get the privilege to go all the way with it because we enter into deeply committed relationships at a young age. And, of course, we're always changing as we get older. However, I think it's very important to lay down the **basic foundation** of who we are before pursuing any type of long term, committed relationship.

This is one of the reasons couples who marry at a young age rarely last. Did you know that the divorce rate for high school sweethearts is over 60% within 15 years? One of the main reasons why is because neither partner has fully discovered who they are. More importantly, they haven't taken the time to love who they are. So, taking the time to know yourself, discover yourself, and then love that self are very important for you, but it's also important to any future relationships.

Look at it From the Other Way Around

If you met a man who was unsure of himself or who had an obvious dislike for himself, could you love him? It's possible that you could, but let's be honest, wouldn't his insecurities turn you off? Wouldn't his insecurities lead to jealousy on his part? Who wants to be around that on a consistent, long-term basis?

This is what happens to us when we've not taken the time to be sure of who we are. We can become insecure, jealous, overbearing, needy, and/or clingy. When we've taken the time to know who we are and be sure of who we are, we don't become threatened by other women. We know in our hearts that we're awesome so there's never a need to become jealous or insecure.

We also won't put up with disrespect or allow ourselves to get involved with men that display bad habits, such as cheating or looking at other women. We just won't tolerate it. When a man knows you won't tolerate crap, he won't bring crap your way. He will have respect for you, simply because you've learned to love and respect yourself first and foremost.

Have you ever really liked a man that was an asshole? Perhaps you've loved an asshole? He was a jerk, but he sure turned you on. That's because one thing about assholes is that they love themselves. They don't care about what you or anyone else thinks about them. They're self-serving, self-loving, and confident. This is a very sexy trait. You can develop this same trait, (without being an asshole), simply by loving yourself first and foremost.

When you take time to yourself, to first find out who you are, and then you learn to truly love who you are, eventually you will develop the "I don't give a fuck what anyone thinks" attitude. You may be one of the lucky women who was born with this attitude. If so, be thankful, not everyone is as blessed to be naturally self-loving and confident. Some women have to develop this attitude. Some women may never develop this attitude and they will suffer for it.

Some women develop it after years of being in bad relationships. They finally say, "Enough is enough" and begin living for themselves. But, wouldn't it be awesome to learn this attitude at a young age? To not have to learn it through trial and error?

Spend time being a single, free, self-serving, self-loving woman. Date yourself for a few years. Be your own boyfriend. Love yourself and every part of your unique personality, and be unforgiving about it. Then you will have developed that sexy attitude that no human being can resist. Getting to know yourself is just one of many important aspects of the power of staying single.

Enjoying Freedom

Another reason why staying single is so important is because you need to have a dedicated time in your life when you're free. If we take this time to ourselves at least once in our life, we will avoid the need to go out and pursue it later when we're in a committed relationship. Or even a worse, while in a marriage.

How many times have you heard of a man or woman leaving a relationship because they'd been with the person since they were very young and never felt they had the chance to be free and single? These people devastate their partners when they come to this realization. Unfortunately for the partner that is blindsided, they have put in years or even decades of their life into this person, only for the person to wake up one day and crave freedom and independence.

Men and women alike have been known to walk out in pursuit of the single life, or even worse in pursuit of another person. It's not fair to the partner that gets the shaft. That's exactly why we should all take the time to be single and enjoy freedom.

I'm thankful and lucky that I left to discover myself when I was very young. I got to enjoy the single life. I dated different kinds of men and discovered which qualities I liked and which qualities I didn't like in a man. By the time I did settle down with the man I married and had kids with, I knew that he was exactly what I wanted. I was ready to fully commit for a lifetime. I had no unsettled urges. I think my husband is blessed to know that his wife is not going to wake up one day and decide she wants to be single and free, as she's already been down that road.

No one goes into a marriage expecting to fail, but we cannot predict the future and sometimes people change. Avoid this issue on your end of the relationship by taking time in your life to be single, free, and independent. Then, when you're ready to pursue a commitment, look for men who have done the same.

Men are a lot better than us at utilizing the power of staying single. They've become very good at embracing the single life, taking time for themselves, and enjoying their freedom while it lasts. We can learn a lot from them and we should strive to be more like them in this area. When both men and women take the time to enjoy being single, as well as take the time to learn who they are, independent of others, then the world will begin to see healthier relationships and lower divorce rates.

The problem is that it's natural for us to crave companionship, especially when we're younger. We see everyone else getting boyfriends and settling down with their long term loves. We don't want to be all alone with no one to snuggle with, no one to love us unconditionally. So we seek out committed relationships at a very young age, before we're emotionally mature enough to handle them. There's one huge reason why we do this... fear.

Overcoming Fear

One of the hardest parts about staying single is overcoming fear. Fear's a strong emotion and it comes in many forms to distract and destroy us on our journey through life. When it comes to the power of staying single, fear likes to confuse you and trick you into settling.

It's the classic fear of being alone. The fear of being the only girl without a boyfriend. It's the dreaded fear of the quiet loneliness. It's the fear that something is wrong with you because you don't have a boyfriend. The fear of having to go out by yourself.

The list of fears that push us to seek out commitments at a young age could go on and on, and they're different for each person. We need to be able to recognize these fears. More importantly, we need to ask ourselves if fear is pushing us to commit to the wrong person at the wrong time in our lives.

I'm thankful that I woke up one day and recognized what I was doing. I recognized that I was afraid and that fear was holding me back from being myself. I was afraid of a lot of other things too. When I first committed at the very young age of fifteen, I was afraid of being the only girl without a boyfriend. Later, I was afraid that if my boyfriend and I broke up that I would never find another guy I clicked with. However, I had to let the fear go. I had to grow up and become a woman, an independent woman.

During my single years, I overcame all of my fears. I came to learn that they were ridiculous fears with no merit. For every fear, there was a flip side to it that was empowering and refreshing. Who cares if I'm the only one without a boyfriend? I'm the only one that's free! And the whole fear of never finding another connection with a guy? Well, I found a much deeper connection with a man that treated me ten times better and totally cracked me up.

Now's the time to ask yourself some serious questions. Is fear holding you back from making important life decisions? Is fear keeping you from not truly being yourself? Is the fear of being alone sabotaging your journey of self-discovery? Take this time to analyze what kind of role fear is playing in your life. Then take the time to look at the flip side of these fears. How can setting the fear aside and embracing the things you're afraid of actually bring positivity, joy, and empowerment into your life?

Doing Things for Yourself

Every woman should take time out of her life to do something special for herself. Whether it's one big treat, like a vacation, or several small treats, like pedicures and new clothes. Some of you may not have this problem and may feel thoroughly spoiled. However, a lot of us (myself included) ignore our own wants and needs. We put ourselves on the back burner and other people's needs are more important.

If you're single and without kids, this is much easier to do. So, you should do it now, while you can. You don't want to look back and feel foolish for not putting your needs as a priority when you had the chance. If you think you can't do it now, try doing it with a family and a stack of monthly bills. That's when it really becomes difficult.

If you're like me and you have a hundred different reasons for not putting yourself first, try to figure out a way around it at least once in a while. Make it happen for yourself. Do whatever it takes to treat yourself to something nice. Every human being should take the necessary steps to spoil themselves at least once in a while. We all deserve a break, an occasional treat, or some extra help.

If you don't stop every once in a while and do something selfish, you're going to look back on your life and regret it. I will use myself as a brief example. For whatever reason, my parents never got me braces. As I grew into adult hood I always thought about getting them but always assumed that I couldn't afford it. My assumptions were wrong. At the age of 27, I found out that braces had been within my financial reach all along. By the time I was 29, I had them paid off and I had a new, beautiful smile.

I often sit back and wonder why it took me so long to get those damn braces. Was I that cheap? Did I not care about myself enough to make that small financial sacrifice? I wish I would've been selfish enough to worry about myself when I was younger. If you're like me, and you put yourself on the back burner for whatever reason, take some time and money to do something important for yourself.

Maybe it's braces. Maybe you would like to hire a maid once in a while. Perhaps, a quick get away with your best friend. Maybe it's even something as simple as new makeup, clothes, or a purse. Or, maybe it's something more meaningful like going back to school, changing careers, or getting in shape. Whatever it is, figure it out and go do it for yourself.

You're worth it!

No one is going to take care of you but you. No one is going to demand that you spoil yourself. You have to make that demand by doing it yourself. The easiest time to get away with it is while you're single. So, if you're single, take advantage of this time in your life and use the power of staying single as an excuse to spoil yourself.

Commitment Being Your Choice

The number one most empowering aspect of the power of staying single is the fact that commitment becomes your choice. It's no longer a man's decision. It's no longer up to him when you're going to commit. The decision is yours. There's so much power in commitment being your choice that it literally changes the game when it comes to dating.

Choosers are never beggars. No longer are you the one seeking out relationships and commitment. The power of staying single goes hand in hand with the power of being the game because now men are chasing you. They're asking you to spend time with them, and begging you to settle down and commit, not the other way around.

This is especially important for women who desire the classic romance story. The ones who desire a man that pursues them, falls in love with them, and gets down on one knee to propose to them. It's the women that make men chase them for commitment that have men begging for their hand in marriage.

People want what they can't have; especially men. When you don't give your heart away easily, it becomes a hot commodity, full of value. On the other hand, when you're too eager for commitment, it can come off as desperation. Who likes to buy things from desperate people? No one. It's an automatic turn off.

So, lie low, stay single, learn to love yourself, spoil yourself, and don't settle down too easily. When you utilize the power of staying single, you will be able to utilize several other powers of womanhood previously discussed in both books. It's a very important part of being a young woman in today's world.

If you're single you should make it a goal to stay single for a few years. That way when you meet the man that is to be your future husband, and he proposes to you, he will feel extra special. He will be honored knowing that getting you to commit was a special thing only he was able to accomplish.

This needs to be a major part of your dating dynamics. Men are supposed to chase us down for commitments, but somewhere along the way we forgot the order of courtship. Nowadays, women are the ones hunting down men and begging the men to settle down. This is not the normal order of operations when it comes to relationships. The power of staying single will change all of that and put the power back in your hands.

Chapter Three

The Power of Being a Woman of Integrity

Whether it's love, sex, or just playful lust... it's disrespectful to be a mistress, girlfriend, side chick or fuck buddy with a man who's married or in a committed relationship with another woman. There's no other way to say it and there's no excuse to justify it. And yes, I know that there are times when men lie about their wife and kids and trick us into relationships. However, for the purposes of this chapter, I'm speaking directly to the women who intentionally get into relationships with married or committed men.

If you're currently in this situation, or you're a woman that finds herself dealing with these kind of issues time and time again, this chapter is for you. I'm going to discuss why being a woman of integrity is imperative. I'm going to explain why it's powerful for you and women everywhere.

Being the other woman is obviously disrespectful to the wife, girlfriend, and/or children involved, but more importantly, being the other woman is disrespectful to **YOU**. You're selling yourself short, and no woman should ever sell herself short for a man. Every woman should carry herself as a woman of integrity, a woman of morals and high standards. Don't be a man's side piece of ass. Don't do that to yourself. That's the most disrespectful and powerless position to be in.

Of course, the men are just as responsible (if not more) for their wrong doings, but that doesn't excuse the woman's part in it. Remember, we cannot control what men do, but we can control what we do. If women were not willing to be participants, then all of the negative behavior would fall on the men.

There are a lot of women who don't have this issue. They've set boundaries and will not get involved with men who are in relationships. If you're one of these women, kudos to you for doing the right thing and for being a woman of integrity. We should all hold ourselves to high standards and make a commitment to each other that we will not partake in this devious type of behavior. There are three important reasons why every woman should commit to being a woman of integrity.

#1) Pussy Power Devaluation

#2) Karma is a Cunt

#3) Camaraderie Between Women

Pussy Power Devaluation

When there are too many women willing to sleep with men in relationships... let me re-phrase that and put it more bluntly... when there's too much free pussy going around, it devalues the entire market. Pussy power everywhere loses value. It's just too accessible. If *every* woman made a personal promise to *never* have inappropriate relations with married or committed men, then a lot of this unethical nonsense would stop.

Sure, there's always hookers and strip clubs and if a man's gonna cheat, then he's gonna cheat, but it sure would make it a lot harder. Especially if women everywhere rejected the notion. If we all led by example and taught our daughters, nieces, sisters and other young girls that look up to us that we do not stoop to low levels for men, then over time, through generational and social conditioning, the lies and games would stop.

It would cease to exist because there would be no women left to participate. Even if just the women who read this book made that promise, it would probably be enough to see a significant increase in our collective pussy power.

So, not only is being a mistress degrading to you, it's degrading to our collective pussy power. We devalue the pussy stock market when we sleep with married and committed men! We must all vow to stop doing this to one another. If you're a woman reading this book, and you've not already decided that you will never disrespect another woman like that, then take this moment to make that commitment.

And if you're currently having an affair, and you've already decided that you hate the wife or girlfriend, then perhaps you don't care. You probably couldn't care less about "that bitch" or whether or not you're disrespecting her. If that's the way you feel, then you're probably letting the advice about pussy power devaluation go in one ear and out the other. That's fine. Every woman is entitled to her characteristics and opinions. But, before you judge her so hastily... picture this...

You've got her out of the picture for good. You've finally got your man all to yourself. Life is great for the both of you now that she's finally moved on with her life. You finally feel that you've found your soul mate, and you're both deeply in love. He proposes. You have your dream wedding, buy a house, and maybe even have some babies. Over the years, you create a beautiful family.

He loves you, cherishes you, and treats you like a queen. Time goes by and you're growing old together, all while watching your kids grow up. You've been together for 20 years. Then one day his behavior begins to change. One day he loves you and the next day he just seems to act different.

Then it happens. Everything you built with your man all comes crashing down the day you find out that your soul mate, lover, husband, and the father of your children has been having an affair behind your back. After months of broken promises, lies, and drama he makes an announcement. He's leaving you for his mistress.

How would that make you feel? Put yourself in a wife's shoes. I mean literally take one minute to feel the emotions and the devastation of what that does to a woman. How would you feel to give your love and life to someone, only to one day down the road have them cheat on you or leave you for another woman? How could any woman ever do that to another person and still be able to sleep at night?

Karma is a Cunt

Having sex with another woman's man is bad karma. Karma is real. Everything that you do now, whether good or bad, will come back to you tenfold. It may not happen now. In fact, it always happens when you least expect it. You don't have to believe in karma. Karma believes in you. It will come for you whether you believe in it or not.

You don't want to do that to your future self. Don't allow present-day mistakes to haunt you in your future. You don't want to find yourself as an older woman—married with children and perfectly content—only to wake up one day and see it all destroyed by infidelity.

Camaraderie Between Women

Ladies... where's the camaraderie? Why do we hate each other so much? Men stick together. Why can't we do the same? Men high five each another when they fuck the same girl. Then they go have a beer and laugh about it while they call her a dirty slut.

We, on the other hand, take that shit to extremes, ready to kill a bitch and scratch out her eyeballs. All for some dick. We blame the other woman instead of blaming the real culprit: the cheating man. Why can't we just high five one another and move on like the men do?

We need to have more fellowship between women. If we all come together for the sake of one another, life will be so much better for all of us. It's only because there are women out there willing to sleep with married men that infidelity is allowed to persist. Don't be that woman.

I don't care how much you love that man. I don't care how much he makes your heart sing. Don't do that to your fellow woman. There are too many men in this world to be sharing or fighting over any of them!

Why?

If you're currently having an affair or you keep ending up in relationships with committed men, you need to take this time to dig deep into your subconscious and ask yourself, "Why do I keep doing this?" Search long and hard until you can come up with a true and heart-felt answer. There's a reason why you're doing this. A reason beyond the basic and simple explanations of "I love him" or "His wife's a bitch." Some examples of the deeper reasons why might include:

- Anger, hatred, or mistrust towards other women
- Anger, hatred, or mistrust towards men
- Being raised by people or in an environment that taught you it's okay or normal behavior to sleep with married or committed men
- Low self-esteem, not feeling worthy of your own committed man
- Believing the myth that all the good men are married or taken
- Financial gains or security
- Enjoying the high or thrill that comes along with pursuing another woman's man
- Fulfilling your ego

The Ego High

There's one huge problem with the last two reasons that should never be overlooked. One of the reasons women find themselves in these situations is due to the ego high. When a man makes you feel that you're better than his wife or girlfriend, this gives you a ***feeling of superiority.*** This feeling of superiority is giving you a temporary high. It's like a drug and it can be very addicting and exciting.

We like to ignore this issue or be in denial about it so we can continue on the fun adventure of stealing another woman's man. If we admit to ourselves that we're just doing it all for the thrill of being better, then the party's over... and we don't want the fun to end. The same way addicts don't like to admit they have a problem because then they have to do something about it (like quit). By being in denial we can keep feeding the ego the superiority it loves, rather than admitting it's all just a thrilling game we're playing at the expense of deeply hurting others.

Feeding the ego with a power trip is like giving a crack head some crack. A crack head doesn't care who he hurts in the process or what kind of evil things he has to do to get his fix. As long as he gets his dope and can get high in the end, he's happy and couldn't care less about anyone's feelings.

A woman that feeds into the high of being a mistress is similar to an addict. She's chasing a temporary euphoria and she's not concerned with who her actions are affecting in the long run. Even when it's affecting her own self-worth and causing damage to her own life.

Don't feed into the addiction of the ego high. It could be an addiction to a particular man because he's just so good at making you feel like the most beautiful and special woman in the world. It could be an addiction to stealing men that belong to other women because it makes you feel like you're so fucking bad ass that you can get a man to leave his wife or girlfriend. You may even be the type that enjoys the chase because it's thrilling and stimulating. Then, once you have the man all to yourself or have destroyed their relationship, you quickly lose interest. However it plays out for you, if you're one of these women, stop and ask yourself if you're feeding an addiction to an ego high with this behavior.

But, I Love Him

Most women who are having an affair with a married man are going to say a few classic things: "But we really love each other. You just don't understand. We have a connection. We're soul mates. His wife just doesn't get him the way I do. He can't stand her, and besides she can't satisfy him the way I do." Sound familiar? Are these the lines you defend your affair with? That's okay. I believe you.

However, if he really and truly feels this way about you, have enough respect for yourself and your fellow woman to back off and let him prove it to you. He can prove it by divorcing his wife or leaving his girlfriend for good. You can remain a woman of integrity by refusing to continue the relationship until the old relationship has been officially finalized. If your love is really true, you will easily be able to re-kindle the romance when there is a blank slate. However, if it's just a relationship based off of sex, lies, and ego highs, then be prepared to lose to the wife.

Besides, aren't you worth it? Aren't you worth having him all to yourself? If you're really as awesome as he says you are, then you're not the kind of girl that needs to share a man... are you? If you're really as amazing as he says you are and his wife is really as bad, boring, or bitchy as he says she is, shouldn't he be able to leave her for you, for good? Shouldn't the choice be easy? The process may not be easy, but the *choice* should be easy.

Don't fall into the mistress trap. Don't disrespect yourself like that. You don't deserve to be any man's side chick. You don't deserve to sit around waiting for him to spend his time with you at his convenience. You're an amazing, beautiful woman and you deserve the title of girlfriend or wife. You deserve to be introduced to his family as his woman, not hidden away from them or looked down upon by them. You deserve a normal relationship with a man that has 100% dedication to you.

Don't confuse the "high" of stealing another woman's man with love. Those good feelings you get when he's telling you how sexy you are, or how much better than his wife you are, are not feelings of love. It's just sweet nothings whispered in your ear. Those lines are only good for stimulating your ego and getting into your pants. It gets you all happy and feeling good in the short term, but like every high, you always have to come back down to reality. That reality of when he walks out of the door after that wonderful night and goes home to his wife... while you're left sleeping all alone.

If a man is not willing to wipe the slate clean and start new with you, the reality is that you're just a side piece. A quick and easy fuck. You're being used. You give him what he wants, when he wants it, and all he has to do is spit game in your ear. For the love of God, don't fall for that crap! Don't be that girl.

The Test

You know deep down inside it's wrong, but if you must defend your actions with the "But it's true love and we have a connection" excuse, then test him. I don't even think you should test him, because what you're doing is wrong regardless, but if you must persist, here's a test to help you decide. The next time you're together in an intimate setting, don't do anything sexual. Tell him you just want to spend time cuddling and talking.

Then, do the same thing for the next three times you're

together. And of course, don't tell him he's being tested. That would be cheating. If he truly loves you for you, then he will be happy to oblige. He won't get pissed off, agitated, impatient, or threaten to leave. Test him to see if he's only in it for the sex. Don't make having sex with you an easy thing to achieve, and see how fast his sweet compliments turn into complaints.

If a man truly loves you, then he will divorce his wife or leave his girlfriend for good before he has any more contact with you. If you set that demand and he fulfills it, then you know it was meant to be. However, if he dances around the idea and comes up with a million and one excuses as to why he can't leave her, then you know where his heart stands. It doesn't stand with you. It stands with her or his family. Perhaps he no longer loves her, but he loves the idea of his family staying together more than he loves you, or he would leave.

You don't know for certain that what he's telling you is the truth. He could be telling her every night how much he loves her and cherishes her, and meanwhile telling you he can't stand her fat ass. He's playing both of you like a fiddle. He tricks each of you into believing the other one is the only fool in the triangle.

You're nobody's fool. You're worth more than being someone's toy or game. You're worthy of a relationship with a man that's going to be there for you 100% of the time, not one that has to share his time and split it up amongst women. It's just not worth it. Besides, 95% of the time, the side chick will be the loser in the end.

Don't Learn the Hard Way

Too often we learn the hard way that this type of behavior usually leads to heartache, pain, and years wasted on broken promises. Older and wiser women may tell you to back off, but you ignore their warnings. It's not until years have passed and he's still with his wife and kids, or he's broken your heart for the last time, that you finally realize everyone was right. Now you're the older and wiser woman turning to younger women and warning them of the same consequences. It's a bad cycle of live and learn.

Don't learn the hard way. Be smart. Think wisely. If a man can't handle staying faithful to his wife or family, what makes you think he will suddenly turn into a man of morals for you? If he's weak enough to compromise his ethics for some pussy, he cannot handle being a good, quality man. Not for his wife or girlfriend, and certainly not for you.

He has no integrity. He has no self-control. Do you really believe deep-seated personality traits like these can be reversed? If he did it then, odds are that he'll probably do it again.

An Open Letter to the Mistresses from Your Fellow Woman:

This letter is to all of the women that reject this advice because they "do what they want." It's for all the women that could give a fuck about what I or anyone else thinks. To the women who have a contest mentality about this subject, thinking "May the best woman win." May I remind you that your behavior is affecting the entire female species as a whole? When you degrade yourself, you are degrading me. You are degrading your mother, your friends, and your daughters.

You're setting a bad example of what a woman is, and an even worse example of what she deserves. We all represent each other and we need to have each others' backs. Men stand up for each other and cover for one another. We turn our backs on each other and stab one another in the back. We pretend to be a friend to a woman and then fuck her man behind her back. Sure, there are men out there that are deceitful and they don't all stick together, but men sure have a much better way of handling these situations than we do.

Ladies, we need to get it together. Let's stop hating one another. Let's respect one another. When we respect ourselves and respect one another, the men of this world will have no choice but to respect us and remain faithful.

Instead we do this dumb shit: fighting over men, stealing men away, getting pregnant by married men, ruining our friendships, and sabotaging relationships for the joy of it. In the end it only makes us look desperate and pathetic. Fighting over some dick?! Are any of us really that desperate? And is a cheating, unfaithful hoe of a man really ever worth it? Pfft.

A Man of Integrity

If his morals and integrity are so low that he would cheat on his wife or girlfriend, what kind of human being do you think he is? A worthy man? An honest man? Do you really think that you're just so damn fine and wonderful that your awesomeness is what made this man cheat and become corrupted? Please. If he did it with you, he will do it with the next sexy woman who's foolish enough to compromise her morals.

If you're lucky, then he won't leave his woman for you and he will break your heart or cut you off and go back home. If you're unlucky, then he will leave his woman for you and you can have him all to yourself and he will turn around and do the exact same thing to you. People of low morals rarely change from circumstance to circumstance. It's who they are in their core being. They either have integrity about these things or they don't. Don't you want a man of integrity?

It's a fact of life: people can fall out of love and couples sometimes fall apart, but a man with integrity will finish the relationship with his current woman before moving on to the next one. He will have enough respect for his current woman to bring that relationship to a close before embarking on the next one. And if he's an intelligent man he will take some time in between relationships to gain closure and insight into his future. He won't hop from one woman to another.

Not only is it immature, but it's nasty. Who wants a dirty used up man that bounces around from woman to woman? See, men have that type of mentality towards us, when it comes to cheating women, but rarely do we look at men in the same shameful way. Men will speak down upon a woman who sleeps with more than one man, or cheats on her mate. They will degrade her and label her a whore, a slut, a skank, a dirty hoe, etc. But what names do we have for men that cheat? Dogs? Pigs?

Men have it easy. The words used to degrade them are just too easy to get away with. They aren't shameful enough. We need to put more pressure on them. How about from now on we treat cheating men the same way men treat cheating women? We need to start calling them nasty and degrading names. Calling them pigs and dogs just isn't going to cut it anymore.

How about filthy hoes with dirty dicks? Infested dicks. Crusty dicks. Puss filled herpes dicks. Useless lame fucks. Syphilis lickers. Weak ass pussies. Anything that provides the same level of shame that we're dealt. Maybe if we put more emphasis on degrading their bad behaviors, they will begin to feel as much shame as we're made to feel for the same type of behaviors.

They've had it far too easy. From now on let's all start making them feel like dirty sluts. We need to make faces of disgust when we hear about them sleeping around. We need to shake our heads with disapproval. They shouldn't be allowed to get away with simple comparisons to animals. No, they need to feel shame and disgust just like we're made to feel. A man that cheats is a nasty, disease spreading, dirty pervert. He's a weak man. A man of low morals and no integrity.

You should never stoop to that level. Be a woman of integrity. Only involve yourself with men of integrity. Don't participate in the devaluation of women. Serve as a wise mentor to the younger generation, and show them what it means to be a strong woman with moral values. Build camaraderie with your fellow women.

You're a unique, beautiful woman. A valuable treasure for any man. There's no one else like you in this world. Why settle for less? You deserve nothing but the best. Never sell yourself short by sharing a man. Don't give into the games. Don't let the ego high distract you from doing what's right. Don't fall into the trap of a believing it's okay to be a man's mistress or side chick. Not only is it a powerless position to be in, but it reflects badly upon you. And should you choose to ignore this chapter's advice, just remember... karma is a cunt.

Chapter Four

The Power of Choosing Your Battles

Behind every great man is an even greater woman... nagging him to death. Ladies, let's be honest for a moment. We like to complain. Well, maybe we don't *like* to complain, but we *have* to complain. Complaining is a necessity when dealing with men. How else will they remember to take out the trash? How else will they remember to fold the clothes, change the baby's diaper, or make sure the kids take a bath?

If it weren't for the nagging of a woman, a lot of men wouldn't get shit done. Plain and simple. They would sit around in their underwear, scratching their balls, while playing Grand Theft Auto Five for thirteen hours straight. Which always sounds like a good idea to them until they realize they're lonely, horny, hungry, and slowly turning into an unambitious, useless loser. They need our nagging because they need our nurturing. Women motivate men.

It all goes back to the power of that pussy! Do you think men would listen to half of what we have to complain about if they didn't need to get that pussy? They wouldn't care. Pussy is a motivator, and unfortunately for them, pussy comes along with some demands and expectations (or at least it should). Expectations such as not being a loser, being a hard worker, remaining faithful, and being a good husband.

Of course there are self-motivated men that work hard with or without the nagging of a woman. I'm not saying all men are unmotivated. But even these hard working, self-reliant gentleman feel a deep subconscious push to work hard and have nice things because deep down inside they desire to attract women. All of this attraction really boils down to the natural, God given desire to mate.

Pussy makes the world go around. We are very important to existence because we motivate men to get stuff done, but more importantly we're needed to repopulate the world! Think about that the next time you get down on yourself. You're a woman and with that awesome privilege comes a very purposeful position in this world.

So, since our private parts are so motivating, we were unknowingly dealt the ultimate responsibility of being supervisors. Like an employee needs a paycheck and therefore has motivation to do what the boss man says, a man needs his woman, and under the right circumstances, he will do what she says. Nagging is a natural part of our nurturing nature designed to keep the wheels of life turning in a forward motion. It's a necessity and it's a part of our design and that's why we can't help but complain. Sorry guys, but that's just the way we are.

The problem we face as women is that sometimes all of this nagging (or lack thereof) gets us into trouble. The problem we face with this subject is twofold. On one side, some of us nag, fight, and/or complain too much and it causes a lot of unnecessary conflict in our lives. All of this unnecessary conflict can lead you to unintentionally break down your relationship, cause you to be in an unhealthy relationship, or lead you into a life of unwanted solitude. On the other hand, some of us don't complain enough. We don't expect much and therefore we lead a lot of men down a path of slacking off, all while sacrificing our own needs and wants.

It's all about balance. Too much bitching is cause for trouble, but not enough bitching can turn you into a pushover. Either scenario can wreak havoc for a woman and can lead to problems in her relationship. Whether she is casually dating, in a committed relationship, or has been married for 20 years, a woman must use good judgment with her 'motivating powers'.

We must all learn to choose our battles.

This is not to be confused with trying to appease the men in our lives. Choosing our battles is about us. It's about our happiness. The power of choosing your battles will bring positive change into your life, *especially* if you find yourself in any of these scenarios:

~If you find yourself constantly upset and aggravated with

everything your man does.

~If you're chronically single because all of the men you've dated had some kind of issue that's caused you to end up dumping them all.

~If you fight with your man so much that it's driving a wedge in between the both of you.

~If you've ever been told you're a doormat or a pushover.

~If you've ever been told by your man that you love to complain or that nothing he ever does is good enough.

~If you've decided that you're just meant to be single because 99.9 percent of the men you've dated irritated the hell out of you.

~If your man has threatened to leave you because he can't take the fighting or nagging anymore.

~If you allow your man to get away with just about anything.

~If your man has told you that you blow things out of proportion and over exaggerate.

~If you can't think, act, or decide for yourself and it drives your man crazy.

~If you turn mountains into mole hills so much that it's making you or your man miserable.

~If you tell yourself that you would rather face a life of being single than to have to commit to a guy with imperfections.

~If men make you cringe.

~If you make yourself cringe.

All of these situations listed above are good examples of people who will benefit the most from this chapter. I'm going to break this chapter down into four sections: the nagger, the pushover, the fighter, and the perfectionist. As you read through these sections, you may find one that fits you perfectly, or you may see bits and pieces of yourself scattered throughout.

See if you identify with any of the classifications below. If you find that you fit the mold, own it. Then take this knowledge about yourself and use it as an opportunity to learn and grow. Recognizing which category(s) you fit into will help you utilize the power of choosing your battles. Learning to use that power wisely is what will bring balance, happiness, calmness, and stability into your relationship and your life.

The Nagger

I'm a nagger. I will admit it. Most women in long term commitments or marriages are going to end up being naggers. We can't help it. We don't really want to be naggers. It's almost like a call of duty when living with a man. One must nag. However, the difference between the naggers that have long lasting healthy relationships and the naggers that get the boot (or end up leaving their man because they can't nag him enough to elicit a change) are the ones who learn that they must choose their battles.

Choosing your battles doesn't mean you need to settle for less or take shit from anyone. It's just a matter of asking yourself, "Is this worth it? Is whatever I'm mad about worth my energy to nag about it? Is it worth me getting myself upset? Is it worth the fight?" Fifty percent of the time, it's just not going to be worth it.

However, there are those days when we can't help but to

nag. Regardless, we should learn to choose our battles and control the urge to nag *for our own sanity*. See, the power of choosing your battles is not really about them. It's about us. It's about our tranquility in life. It's about our happiness.

So, it's not about bowing down or cowering. It's not about sacrificing our own self-worth or settling for crap. Another reason why is because nagging too much can be a big waste of our time and energy. You know why? Men tune out nagging. The sound that comes out of our mouths when our voice goes from a normal pitch to a nagging pitch is on another frequency.

Man frequency does not pick up the sound waves and we immediately get tuned out. The better way to deal with this issue is to use this knowledge to get what we want, without the need to nag. That is by simply and directly asking for what we want or need, and asking sweetly.

Here we go back to "Just Say It" from book one. But, I'm serious. Men are very direct, one-track-minded people. If you don't have his utmost attention when asking or nagging about something, there's a high chance he's going to forget. Then there's a high chance that you're going to get annoyed and feel disrespected.

It's not that he doesn't love you or respect you. It's not that he's lazy and doesn't want to do it (well, maybe a little bit). He most likely forgot or didn't even process the request the first time because he was thinking about something else. It could also be that because you're asking in a negative way, he automatically gets defensive and then is resistant to cooperate.

The next time you feel the nagging coming on, remind yourself to control the urge and simply ask with kindness. Ask with a smile on your face. You could also try coming from behind him, giving him a big hug and a kiss, and then say whatever it is you would usually nag him about; but say it sweetly and politely. "Honey, would you take the garbage out for me? I would appreciate it so much." If and when he does it, make sure to say thank you. If he doesn't do it immediately, politely remind him in an hour or two.

Give him two chances. If after the second round of niceness he still hasn't obliged, then give yourself permission to nag. I'm not saying you should never ever nag, because I know good and well that sometimes it must be done. However, allow yourself the opportunity to accomplish more and to effortlessly get what you want by remaining cool and calm about it. Then, if you can't kill him with kindness, kill him with the nagging.

However, you will find that when it comes to communicating with your man, you're going to get him to cooperate more by being a sweetheart about it, rather than immediately resorting to nagging. On the plus side, you're keeping your stress levels down by remaining peaceful about the situation. Better yet, if you have kids, you're teaching them by your actions that you can get more of what you want in life by remaining peaceful, cool, calm, and collected.

The Push Over

The push over is on the other end of the spectrum. She needs to learn to stand up for herself. She needs to learn to choose her battles more frequently, rather than allowing her man to run all over her and take advantage of her kindness. You know you're a push over if you let your man get away with murder and you forgive him time and time again. If you're the type of woman that says, "Sure, Babe," when inside you're really thinking, "NO, ASSHOLE!" then you need to use the power of choosing your battles to stand up for yourself. Use this power to help you begin voicing your opinion more freely and frequently.

Being someone's doormat is never going to lead to fulfillment within your relationship. Either you're going to get sick of it or he's going to begin to try and get away with more and more shit over time. Being the "yes girl" can lead to him pushing the envelope a little more each time, until eventually over the span of many years he's just going to do whatever he wants. You're spoiling that man. What happens when someone gets spoiled? They don't appreciate shit. The minute they have to do something they don't want to do they throw temper tantrums, start fights, and run away from the issue.

Being a pushover is like putting your man in training for the big spoiled baby competition, and you're the coach. Don't do that to yourself. You don't want to be a man's mommy. Be his wife. Be his girlfriend. Don't be his maid, butler, waitress, and chef, all wrapped into one. Then after all of that catering, you allow him to have sex on demand. Where is *your* happiness in all of this catering?

You may be thinking, "I'm happy" or "but I love him." But are you really happy or is it just a front? Are you happy with the way you're treated? Are you happy when he leaves to go hang out with other people and leaves you behind? Are you happy when he cheats, yells at you, or treats you like shit and disrespects you in front of people?

You may truly love him and that's okay, but don't allow love to fool you into believing that you're happy, if you're not. If he's taking your kindness for weakness or taking your love for granted, don't lie to yourself about this. If you stay in denial, you'll have no one to blame but yourself for putting up with his shit. You can't blame him. You decide what you will allow by putting up with it. You decide. Not him.

Before you know it, years have gone by, and he gets more and more comfortable while you get more and more complacent. Grow a back bone *before* he gets too comfortable. This doesn't mean you have to turn into a raging bitch. You don't even have to fight or raise your voice. You just need to stand up for yourself more often and become comfortable with voicing your opinion. The power of choosing your battles will help you by getting you to recognize when to speak up and when to let shit slide.

You're going to want to go to battle anytime you feel taken advantage of or disrespected. However, if disrespect is happening on a regular basis, you may need to go to war... by leaving him. Give him a warning that you need things to change for your own happiness, and then give him a chance to change. But if things don't begin to get better, you need to leave him alone for good. You don't deserve to spend your life being someone's doormat.

Now if you're prepared to go to battle and stand up for yourself, but you just don't feel comfortable being that kind of woman, than you need to remember the power of confidence and the power of the pussy. These two powers will help you in this situation. Build up enough confidence to voice your opinion and stand up for yourself. Use the power of the pussy to get your way and to reinforce good behavior.

As I mentioned earlier, this is not about fighting all of the time or becoming a bitch. The power of choosing your battles is important to the push over because it allows her to have a voice. Every woman deserves to have an opinion and stand up for herself. If you're a pushover this may seem difficult to implement due to guilt. Don't feel guilty about this. It's normal to have a voice within a relationship. What's not normal is allowing a man to walk all over you and disrespect you.

If you're really uncomfortable about this, then start off with voicing your opinion about small and stupid things, like what's for dinner. When he asks you where or what you want to eat, instead of giving him the same, "whatever you want, Babe" or "I don't know," actually grow some balls and suggest something YOU like. It's not a big deal. You don't have to allow him to decide everything. You're allowed to have an opinion. It's your God-given right. He may actually appreciate you speaking up and giving suggestions.

Once you're comfortable with voicing your opinion over small things, move on to something a little more complex. When it comes to standing up for yourself over bigger issues, it doesn't have to be dramatic. You can use 'Just Say It'. Remember men are a lot less complex than we are. Stating what you want in a simple yet sweet manner will get you what you want without being a bitch about it.

When the time comes, you may be sitting there nervous as hell about speaking up. What is he going to say? What is he going to do? Is he going to get angry? Then when you finally get the courage to say something, you find him eager to oblige and completely unaware that there was ever even an issue. He might even appreciate that you approached him and communicated with him, rather than allowing it to bottle up inside.

There are some men that prefer a quiet, shy, giving type of girl that caters to their needs. If that is your style, that's great. However, be warned that these same men can become annoyed or agitated when their woman constantly lacks an opinion, a back bone, or doesn't have her own two feet to stand firmly upon. So, in trying to keep him pleased, you may actually end up hurting your relationship by turning him off or irritating him.

Worst of all you're compromising your own happiness. That's never a good idea. So, be nurturing, be shy, and be the giving girlfriend that you enjoy being, but don't go to the extreme of being a completely voiceless, robotic, boring doormat. Remember... what does a door mat do? It just lies there and serves no purpose other than allowing people to walk all over it. That's not who you were destined to be, so get off the floor and don't be afraid to speak up once in a while.

The Fighter

This section is for my girls that love to fight. You know who you are, don't deny it. You get off on fighting, even if you don't like to fight. I know that doesn't make any sense, but continue reading and I will explain the logic behind the woman that doesn't *like* to fight, but *loves* to fight.

There are people in this world that get a high off of fighting. It's not that they enjoy the fight, but rather they enjoy the stimuli, the drama, the resolution, the ego high, or they just love getting their way. There's a reason why some people just love to fight, and if you get two of those people together in a relationship, there's going to be a ton of unnecessary drama and constant fighting.

Are you known for making mountains out of molehills? Does your anger go from zero to ten very easily? Does your man know how to push your buttons? Or do you and your man fight more than the average couple? Do you think that every couple fights on a regular basis and your fighting is normal? If you recognize yourself in the above paragraphs, than you my dear, may be a fighter.

Yes, couples fight, but it's not normal to fight on a regular basis, have huge blow ups, fight over stupid things, or to be constantly on the verge of a fight. What is normal and healthy is to express your anger and have occasional fights within a relationship. This is how couples work through issues and compromise. This is what keeps relationships moving in a forward direction and on a strong path. But, the key word is **compromise.**

The problems come in when the fighting doesn't resolve conflicts and instead becomes excessive, unnecessary, unhealthy, abusive, over the top, and/or addictive. You know when fighting is becoming an unhealthy problem when it begins to destroy your happiness and ultimately your relationship. If your fighting is constant and it's causing you to move away from your partner, rather than being a source of understanding and compromise that brings you both together, you can know for sure that your fighting is unhealthy. If this is an issue in your current relationship or has become a pattern within past relationships, than the power of choosing your battles is going to be a great asset to your life and relationships.

First let's cover why the fighter likes to fight. There are a few reasons why some women (and men) just love to fight, although most will never realize, let alone admit, that they're doing this intentionally. Most will blame the other person for being the cause of the arguments. However, I think mature and intelligent women who are tired of the constant issues brought on by fighting will have enough courage to look inside themselves and analyze if they're possibly the source of the problem.

I also want to mention that if you end up coming to the realization that *you* may be the cause or the common denominator in your drama-filled relationship(s), don't feel bad about it. We're all learning and growing as we go through this thing called life. No one is perfect. We all have issues that we need to acknowledge and work on. It's the people that recognize their imperfections and work hard at overcoming them that will benefit, while the ones who chose to ignore, deny, or blame others will continue to sit and fester in their own problems.

So, why would anyone subconsciously want to fight? Fighting is a negative interaction. Surely no one would *like* to fight? However, there are a few reasons why some people get off on fighting, and these reasons make them more prone to start fights and be in tumultuous relationships. In my opinion the three main reasons for this are the ego, addiction, and attention. You may be a fighter for one of these reasons, a combination, or all three.

Three Reasons the Fighter Likes to Fight

#1) The Ego

Fights brought on by the ego have to do with a variety of factors such as the satisfaction of winning, feeling superior, being a control freak, or just plain being selfish and/or spoiled. You may be one of the many women who fight for this reason because unknowingly you enjoy the feeling of being right, being better, having things go your way, or you simply desire to win all of the arguments, all of the time. If you're more of the spoiled type, you just won't stop until you get your way.

It sucks to fight, but it feels good to win.

You may be prone to choose men that are submissive and allow you to win fights and get your way, and therefore you don't have huge issues with this. On the other hand, you could be the type that bounces from commitment to commitment, wondering why your relationships start out great but always fizzle out due to constant arguing or end in break-ups caused by one huge fight.

People that aren't concerned with the ego high will work with their partner on issues, not allow the issues to consume the relationship. If you're an ego fighter, you may find that as soon as a man doesn't give in to you or if he ever dares once to "put his foot down," you lose interest. You either become turned off from the relationship or slowly over time the ego clashing becomes too much for him to take and he gets turned off from the relationship.

If your ego is sabotaging your happiness and relationships, then learning to choose your battles will lead you off of your path of self-serving, righteousness and unto a path of balance, emotional maturity, and ultimately happiness within your relationships. Begin to take notice of when you're getting ready to go off on a tangent and force yourself to stop and reflect if the fight is about a real issue that needs addressing, or if it's just your ego coming out to play.

If you can begin to control yourself from fighting over dumb shit that doesn't really matter and tell yourself to pull back a bit, then you can begin to pick and choose which battles are worth going to war for and which battles you should simply let go. Try to cut back your fighting by 50%. That is one out of every two fights that you will need to hold back the anger or frustration. This way you save the fighting for issues that truly matter. Issues that are more important to you than just temporarily satisfying your ego, being right, or getting your way.

When all else fails and you cannot contain it, you need to accept that you just need a submissive man that's going to say "Yes, Dear" every time. If you cannot accept being with a submissive man *and* you can't learn to control Ms. Ego from rearing her ugly head, than you will have to accept that you're going to be in constant strife mode with the men you date.

Unfortunately, this usually leads to a lifetime of bouncing from commitment to commitment, with relationships that start off great and passionate but go down the drain after a few months to a few years. If that's how you want it, keep being egotistical, but if you truly desire a long-lasting, deeply committed relationship, than from this moment forward begin to choose your battles and choose them wisely. Give in a little bit. It's not going to kill you to let your man have his way once in a while. It may get under your skin temporarily, but you will get past it and in the long-run you will be a happier woman.

#2) Addiction

Addiction to fighting is a very real problem for some. Although the act of fighting itself is not pleasurable, the chemicals released by your brain when you're fighting can become addicting. When you're under stress and your heart starts pumping, your brain releases adrenaline. Adrenaline gets you going, sending a rush to your system. That's where all the energy in a fight comes from. If the fight goes even further and you start breaking dishes, slamming doors, spewing mean and hateful remarks, or even worse, you begin getting physical with each other, the system steps up another notch and begins to release dopamine.

Here is where the problems begin. Dopamine is your feel-good hormone. I'm not a doctor or a scientist, but I know enough about this hormone to know that when it's released we can feel attentive, bold, risky, brave, excited, and very pleasured. This sudden onset of bravery and boldness is one of the reasons why we say and do stupid things that we regret when we're fighting. More importantly, it's one of the reasons why some people can become addicted to fighting.

This hormone is also released when people take drugs and it's one of the main reasons people become addicted to drugs. So, while the act of fighting itself is not pleasurable, the release and rush you get from the dopamine feels good on a physiological level, and that feeling can become very addictive; just as addictive as drugs.

Adding another level to this problem are the people who have passionate make-up sex directly after a huge blow up. This is a double whammy of dopamine inflicted pleasure. Not only are you getting addicted to the fighting, but you're subconsciously enjoying the intense build up to that huge and satisfying release of an orgasm after all is said and done. That amount of intensity and pleasure has the potential to get any person whimsically addicted. So, the next time you hear someone say, "You're addicted to the drama." You can say, "Yes. Yes, I am."

But, let's be honest. No one wants to be an addict. Especially an anger addict. That's no fun. So, if you think this sounds like you, now you know why you may be prone to constantly fight. With knowledge comes the power to do something about it. It's time to begin to eliminate your addiction so that you can move into a healthy and happy relationship(s). Again, this is going to boil down to you choosing your battles.

When you feel that surge of anger coming over you, that feeling that you know is the precursor to your fights, stop yourself. Walk away from the situation if you must. Take a few minutes to ask yourself if the problem is worth the fight. Choose wisely. You don't have to let everything slide and you especially don't need to go to the extreme of being a pushover, but you do need to learn what is worth fighting for and what is worth letting go.

Over time and with practice you will get better and better at recognizing when you're doing this and you will also get better at being able to control it. When you're able to recognize and control it, you will be amazed at how much calmer and happier you will become. Your relationship will blossom and/or you will move on to a relationship that is healthier and more stable. Choose your battles wisely, or fight and live in chaos. The power is in your hands.

#3) Attention

Another reason why some fighters love to fight is for the attention. This is usually a result of having low self-worth and/or low self-esteem. In some unfortunate cases this low self-worth can stem from childhood abuse. For example, being brought up in an environment where negative attention was the only form of attention or growing up in an environment where there was not proper or healthy amounts of attention.

Children crave attention as they develop and if the child's needs are not met under normal, healthy circumstances the child may feel that he or she is not loved or wanted. This leads to a sense of inadequacy, insecurity, and low self-worth. Even though the lack of love, affection, and healthy interactions is never the child's fault, it's internalized and taken *very* personally.

This may (but not all the time) lead to the child needing to seek out attention, and if that attention comes from negative circumstances, then so be it. This attention-seeking behavior can then flow over into adulthood and wreak havoc in one's relationships. Sometimes it may not even have anything to do with childhood issues. It could be a problem that started in adolescence or adulthood. Everyone needs to feel that they belong and matter to others. When a person doesn't feel that belonging, for whatever reason, it will manifest in attention-seeking behaviors and one of those behaviors can be fighting.

For the attention seeker, fighting makes them feel like they are worth something to someone. Someone cares enough to fight. Even if it's only temporary, that someone is paying enough attention to fight with them and that attention is uplifting. They may feel that the person actually cares and loves them because they are passionate enough about the person to fight with them. So, it gives a twisted sense of love, compassion, and security that leads to euphoria. It doesn't matter if it's an unhealthy way of getting it. They are receiving the love and attention they need.

Feelings of inadequacy or insecurity, no matter where they come from, are deeply rooted in people with low self-worth. A person who has low self-worth interprets interactions with others through a distorted lens. It only makes sense that their methods of gaining attention are through distorted means. It's all an attempt to feel better through eliciting praise, forgiveness, or demanding other people's time and focus. If somewhere along the way they figure out that they can get this through fighting, it becomes a hard habit to break.

If you recognize yourself or your situation in the above paragraphs, don't get down on yourself. Recognizing and accepting our issues is half the battle and no one is perfect. The other half of the battle is learning how to deal with our issues in healthier ways than what we're used to. This may take some work but it's all worth it because it will lead to long-term happiness.

In this situation, this all boils down to having healthy self-esteem and self-acceptance. For some people, confidence and self-love are easy concepts to grasp. For others, they may need to learn, study, and train their way to self-love. We worked on this a lot in book one and if you feel you need additional assistance, there is an ebook I recommended in the first book, that I suggest you read, if you have not done so yet. While you're working on your self-esteem, you can use the power of choosing your battles as a tool to help you avoid unnecessary drama.

The Perfectionist

Are you chronically single because every man you date has some kind of issue that you just cannot get over? You may be a perfectionist if every time you go on a date or enter into a relationship you find yourself saying things similar to these lines: His nose is too big. He smells funny. His clothes are too baggy. He spends too much time with his Mom. His back is hairy. His head is flat. His car is old. He's short. He needs to wax his eyebrows. He didn't open the car door for me. His dick is too small. His dick is too big. His breath stinks in the morning. He has kids. He is breathing.

Does this sound like your conversation with your friends when you're analyzing a new potential mate? Even if it's just one or two complaints? If you can't seem to get over small turn offs and it has left you single and alone time and time again, you may be a perfectionist. Which is fine, if you enjoy being lonely, picky, and self-righteous.

However, if you desire to settle down with a man that lives on this planet... he's going to have some flaws. And the chances are pretty high that they're going to be gross or annoying flaws. Nobody's perfect. Not even you and especially not a man. You're never gonna find him, so give it up or give up on the thought of ever having a relationship with a real man.

There's nothing wrong with having standards and expecting certain traits in the men you date or settle down with. That's why we made the dream man list in book one. The problem is when you let a few small and insignificant things get in the way of developing a relationship with a potentially awesome man... *time and time again*. When you do this you're just sabotaging your own happiness.

Use the dream man list as a guide to not only raise your awareness of what you really want, but to help you remember *what is* and *what is not* important. What if you went on a date with the man you were meant to marry but you didn't accept his invitation to a second date because he didn't automatically pass you the bread at dinner or ask if you wanted another drink?

Now, I know some of you are thinking, "That's so stupid. Who would care about something so insignificant?" Well, if that's your mind-set than you're not a perfectionist and this section is not an issue for you. However, Mrs. Perfectionist is out there and she knows who she is and she knows good and well what I'm talking about. Mrs. Perfectionist, I want you to know that it's okay to have turn offs. I'm not saying you should accept things that you just cannot take. All I'm saying is to analyze if you're being too picky and if it's leading you down a path of loneliness.

Sometimes we can be in denial about this loneliness and proclaim that we are 'single by choice', which is great. We should all be single for a while, but don't lie to yourself for years and allow those years to turn into decades. This can easily sabotage your own happiness and rob you of sharing your awesome life with an equally awesome man... just because he had a hairy back.

I know this all sounds so gross, but you know what I'm talking about. We all do it. We all look around at the men when we're single, and honestly it's hard to find that super sexy, perfect guy. Usually when you do find one he's either married, gay, uninterested, or a player. We can't win. So, we must give up on the search for perfection and accept that men are human beings, just like us, and that means that 100% of them are going to have imperfections.

So again, we must learn to choose our battles. In this case, choosing battles isn't about fights or nagging. For the perfectionist, choosing battles is about learning to accept that any man you date is going to have some gross, annoying traits. Then it's about finding the man whose annoying traits are things you can eventually get past. You have to trade the bad for the good.

So, maybe he's a hairy guy, but he's faithful, and head over heels in love with you. Or perhaps he has acne. But, he slings that dick like a professional, pays the bills on time, and would love you for life... but you will never give him the chance to prove it. Or even worse, he was your soul mate, but you turned him away because he made a simple mistake of not offering you his jacket when you were cold.

You know what you do with these men? You train them. You use your amazing pussy powers and you speak your mind and say, "I love it when a man offers me his jacket when I'm cold, and right now I'm freezing." The chances of that man ignoring your direct message and not offering his coat are slim to none. The chances that he's just clueless and unaware that you're cold and waiting for him to offer his jacket, are much higher.

When it comes to the physical stuff, you can still train him. You just have to wait until you've made him fall in love. That's when you take his ass to the salon and get his back waxed, his eyebrows done, or his gray hairs dyed. That's when you deal with whatever imperfection or irritating thing that he does. Any issue you have with a man can either be fixed, corrected, or taught by using the power of the pussy, and the things that can't be fixed can always be overlooked.

Ask any happily married woman and she will tell you that her husband has annoying or gross attributes. I don't care how sexy her husband is, she will tell you a few things that drive her mad. She will also tell you that she had to get used to his imperfections or correct them over time with her pussy power.

When you fall in love with a man, you begin to look past all of his faults. Suddenly, he's not so gross after all. He is actually quite sexy, perhaps the finest man on the planet, because he loves you and would die for you. Love conquers all, even bad breath. However, you will never get to the point of being able to love a man unconditionally and see past his shortcomings if you won't allow him the opportunity to make you fall in love.

Why Are We So Damn Picky?

As women, we push ourselves too hard to be perfect. We're too hard on ourselves and we're too hard on each other. We cover our imperfections with makeup. We push up our boobs and fake the size of them with $50 bras. We wear spanks to disguise our rolls and cellulite. We wear heels to look taller and sexier. We wear extensions in our hair, dye it, and change its natural texture. We wear tight, uncomfortable clothes. Then we go home and at the end of the day we take it all off and there they are... imperfections on the face, sagging boobs or small cup sizes, cellulite, bellies, stretch marks, and jiggling thighs.

Under all that crap is an imperfect woman who just wants to be loved and accepted for who she is. But that same woman is going to have a hard time finding true love if she's unable to accept that any man she dates will have flaws as well. We have got to stop doing this to each other. Men and women alike. None of us are perfect, but we're all special, and we all deserve love and respect despite our flaws, *and so do men.*

It's okay to want to be sexy and look good. It's okay to want your man to be sexy and look good. However, if seeking perfection is getting in the way of your happiness, you need to look within and ask yourself if you're ever really going to find it? Probably not. So, wouldn't it just be best to look past an imperfection every now and then? I'm not saying you need to marry a Sasquatch, but can you find your perfect Prince Charming and look past his hairy eyebrows?

Choosing Wisely

Now that we've gone over all of the different ways we can sabotage our own happiness, whether it's from being a nag, being too picky, too bitchy, or not being bitchy enough, can you see yourself in any of these scenarios? Acknowledging your faults is half the battle. When you recognize your responsibility within your relationship's issues you can begin to do something about it.

Once you've owned up to your faulty characteristics you can begin to turn things around by choosing your battles. The wisest way of choosing, no matter which scenario you find yourself in, is asking yourself a very simple question, "Is this worth it?"

Is it worth nagging about? Is it worth causing an argument? Is it worth adding another layer of drama to the relationship? Is it worth being alone? Is it worth having my way? ***Is this worth my happiness?*** If you can honestly answer that question you will know when to let shit slide and when to stand up for yourself. You will know when to give in and walk away and when to stick it out and fight.

The power of choosing your battles is not about letting shit slide every time, nor is it about letting men get away with murder. Remember, it's about you. Your happiness. Your sanity. Your relationship(s).

In every good relationship there is compromise. Both people have to give a little or the scales tip too far to one side and the relationship flops. Whether it's from the male or the female, if one person in the relationship is constantly "putting their foot down," causing arguments, or not standing up for themselves, things are going to fall apart eventually over time.

Admitting When You're Wrong

Let's say that your constant fighting has caused a strain on your relationship to the point where your man has one foot out the door. You both love each other very much but the arguments have taken over the relationship and both of you are growing tired of it. As women, some of us are very hard headed and would allow our man to walk away from the relationship, rather than simply apologizing.

He has probably apologized 100 times in 100 different fights, but this is the fight that he refuses to budge on. In the heat of the moment, when he's gathering his stuff to leave, you may be thinking, "Walk away, Asshole. Leave. I don't care." You may even say it out loud to him but deep down inside you're crying, "Noooooo. Don't leave. Stay and work it out." He leaves and slams the door on his way out. That's when the tears go strolling down your face.

You're sitting alone, crying, and wondering if you've finally done it. Have you finally pushed him to the breaking point and killed his love for you? "Oh well. Fuck him," you think to yourself. Ignoring the pain deep down inside that encourages you to apologize and admit you were wrong.

Apologizing and admitting we're wrong is one of the hardest things to do for some of us. I know because I'm one of these women. I'm a headstrong Aries woman. I don't like to apologize to anyone for anything because I'm always right (even when I know I'm wrong). It's taken me years to learn how to humbly say I'm sorry when I'm wrong... and I still struggle with it.

Admitting I'm wrong to anyone, especially my man, causes a burning agitation deep inside my core. It's not until I recognized this fault within my personality that I was able to work on making it stop. I've learned to choose my battles, and for me personally, that means apologizing when I'm wrong and holding back on the nagging.

What does the power of choosing your battles mean for you personally? Do you think that the power of choosing your battles can help you find balance and happiness in your life? Do you think that you can relieve stress in your life by holding back some of the time? Can you learn to admit when you're wrong and apologize? Can you cut back on fighting and/or nagging by 50%? Can you learn to stand up for yourself if you're a pushover? Can you learn to overlook imperfections?

If you can begin to choose your battles and choose them wisely, a whole new world awaits you. A world with less stress, less bullshit, less fighting, less anger, less loneliness, and less sadness awaits you. We're women, and very rarely are we ever wrong, but sometimes, *some very, very rare times...* we are.

Recognize your faults and wrong-doings. Work diligently on correcting them. Then sit back and watch your love life slowly change for the better.

Chapter Five

The Power of Food, Sex, and Loyalty

Please note:
The information contained in this chapter is only for women who are in deeply committed relationships with <u>loyal, dedicated, quality men</u>. This information is not to be used on men you've just met, men you've only been dating for a short period of time, new relationships, or unworthy men.

How To Keep a Good Man by Your Side for Life

Now that you've got your dog on a leash, this is how you keep him in the yard for life. If he's a good man and worthy of your love, then you should never feel bad about being a good woman to him. If he treats you like a queen, then treat him like a king. Great relationships are built on mutual respect. A lot of relationships don't work out because the respect isn't mutual. Either the man is very good to the woman and she's not being appreciative of it, or the woman's the one spoiling the man and he's not being appreciative of it.

However, as a woman it's important to remember the first twelve powers. You don't go around spoiling just any man. You make a man prove he's worthy of your affections before you give him your heart and everything wonderful that comes along with it. You must allow a man to court you so that he can show you who he is and who he's going to be in the relationship. Once you feel you've found a winner, then allow the spoiling to begin.

Spoiling a man isn't hard. Spoiling a woman is hard. So, luckily for us, there isn't much you have to do to keep a good man happy, dedicated, and loyal for life. It all boils down to three very basic needs: food, sex, and loyalty. That pretty much sums it up. As basic as that sounds, that's about the extent of what it takes to make most men happy.

I'm going to cover each of these topics separately in a minute. However, first I want to make it clear that all men are different. Some will love food more than others, some will appreciate loyalty more than others, while some will prefer sex over all things. Of course, every man is an individual and his wants and needs will be different from the next man. However, it's important as a woman to simply be aware of how easily satisfied most men are going to be to have regular sex, good food, and dedicated loyalty from the woman they love.

Now hold on. Before some of you get angry and tell me that this is sexist, please remember, I don't sugar coat things and I'm not here to be politically correct. I'm here to be honest with you. Men like to eat and fuck. That doesn't mean you have to be a chef, nor does it mean you have to be a porn star. They aren't seeking perfection.

They're seeking something very basic: nurturing.

We desire men that provide and protect. Does that make us wrong? Does that make us sexist? No. It's in our DNA. Since the beginning of time the man went out and hunted (provided) and the woman cooked the catch (nurtured). Deny it and call it sexist all you want, but it won't change human behaviors that have existed since the beginning of time.

Of course roles have been reversed in many instances. Not every couple is going to fall into this general rule. That's awesome. We should all do what makes us happy. We should all do what works for our individual needs and desires. If you hate cooking and you've found a man that loves to cook, that's great. You found a dynamic that works for you.

However I've found that *in general*, men enjoy being nurtured by the woman they love. They just want to be loved. Love for them comes in very simple terms: Feed me. Fuck me. Appreciate me. Don't give my pussy away to anyone else.

It's very simple. It's very easy. But more importantly, it will keep a good man dedicated to you for life.

It's not sexist. It's not insensitive to our needs. Ignoring these basic natural desires is insensitive to a man's needs. It's the same as a woman being in a relationship with a man that doesn't listen to her, doesn't provide a shoulder for her to lean on, or doesn't protect her. We would say that man is being insensitive to his woman's needs. So, why is it okay for us to expect our needs to be met, but become offended when men are honest about their needs?

When Food, Sex, and Loyalty Doesn't Work

Many of you may be thinking, "I spoil my man. Why's he still an asshole?" Remember, spoiling has to be mutual. You don't go around having great sex and cooking good food for a man who treats you badly or doesn't appreciate it. Now if you've got a good guy that's head over heels in love with you, spoil him, and watch how the mutual love and respect grows exponentially over the years. Couples that do this to one another become those couples that make you sick, because they're so in love, always happy, and rarely fight.

However, some of you may have been spoiling the wrong men or have been spoiling men without even realizing it. It's your natural way of being. You like to take care of your man. There's nothing wrong with that. You just have to remember that this is a special gift you're giving. You don't go around giving special gifts to just any man, let alone an unappreciative man, or a man that *expects* you to do it.

The problem with these situations, whether you're currently spoiling an unappreciative asshole or you find yourself automatically inclined to spoil men and it hasn't worked out for your benefit; is that you've been spoiling the wrong men, at the wrong times! Remember, don't spoil just any man, especially one you've just started dating. Always make sure a man deserves it and always make sure that he is being <u>equally giving to you</u>. Now that you understand when it's worth your efforts, why it's worth your efforts, and why you shouldn't feel bad about doing this, let's discuss the three factors of keeping a good man.

FOOD

Why do you think the quickest way to a man's heart is though his stomach? Is it because men are pigs, and pigs will eat anything? Is it because men are dogs, and dogs love to eat? There are some very basic and simple reasons why men love a woman that cooks and I touched on this earlier. It's the same reasons why we love a hardworking man that provides. It all goes back to our primitive roles when man was the hunter and woman was the caretaker.

As much as all of that's true, I'm still going to get some hate mail telling me that I'm a sexist bitch for assuming women should cook for a man. Please allow me to defend myself. I'm not saying anyone has to learn how to cook. If you don't cook, that's your prerogative.

A lot of women hate cooking. A lot of men love cooking. My father and step-mother happily held this dynamic in their marriage. In some families, both the man and the woman are the chefs in the family and in others neither person wants to cook. There's nothing wrong with any of that. It's about what works for your relationship. It really all boils down to breaking bread together. Who bakes the bread is not important.

However, I'm not going to lie to you. Knowing how to cook, but more importantly how to cook *really well,* is a secret weapon of love! Don't feel inferior for cooking for a man, but don't feel obligated to cook for a man either. It's your choice of when, where, how, what, why or why you're not going to cook for anyone. Let the choice be yours. So, now that I've thoroughly defended my so-called "sexist views" on cooking a good meal for a man, let's talk about this secret weapon of love.

Knowing how to cook is a skill. If you're talented with this skill, use it to your benefit. Use it wisely. You keep that secret weapon at bay until the man in your life has earned a nice meal, and when he has, you cook him the best damn food he's ever eaten. If you do this, that man will be so blown away and honored that it will make his heart sing. (You can even do it half-naked, with a thong on, if you really want to fuck with his head!)

No one is born knowing how to cook. If you feel that you don't know how to cook, don't worry, cooking is a skill that any person can learn. Everyone had to learn from someone else at some point in their lives. Don't let anyone's great cooking skills intimidate you. The only reason older women know how to cook so well is because they've had years of practice.

Take cooking classes if you don't have anyone to teach you, or find recipes that you enjoy. You don't even have to cook all of the time. I don't cook often, but when I do, I make sure it's good and it keeps the bellies I fill full and happy. I intentionally learned to cook at a young age so that I could take care of myself, but also to nurture my future husband and children. I wanted my husband to say, "I love my wife's cooking." I wanted my children to say, "I love my Mom's cooking."

Remember, this isn't about being a man's servant or a slave to the kitchen. **It's about nurturing the man you love.** It's about spoiling him because he spoils you. It's about mutual love and respect. People that know how to cook have a unique way of being able to show love through food, and that's by nurturing with nourishment. Granted, it makes some of us fat, but those extra calories can be worked off by following the advice in the next section.

SEX

Just because you're in a relationship doesn't mean you've forfeited your pussy power! Follow the tips in this section and you'll have a loyal puppy dog by your side for life. Do this for your own benefit, but more importantly as a way of rewarding him for being such an awesome man. It's the power of appreciation manifested through sex! If he's a good man, then he deserves it, right?

We all know men love sex, so using sex to keep a good man happy won't be very difficult, but there are a few things to remember. First things first, when you're in a long-term committed relationship, it can be easy to slip into a boring routine. Be aware of that problem and avoid it by remembering to periodically catch him off guard with something unexpected.

Not only will that keep things exciting, but more importantly, it provides you with leverage. That leverage should be used to make him work for it once in a while. It should also be used for positive reinforcement and pussy negotiations. (See The Power of the Married Pussy)

#1)
Don't be afraid to tell him what you like.

Nine times out of ten, a man is more interested in making his woman reach an orgasm than reaching it himself. ***It turns your man on, to turn you on.*** A good man that loves and adores his woman wants to please her. He wants to know what you like and don't like. Never be afraid to tell your man what turns you off and what turns you on. Not only will this make sex better for the both of you, but it's important to the emotional side of the relationship because it builds intimacy and trust.

#2)
Don't be afraid to use a vibrator during sex. It makes sex better for you, and when you're turned on, it makes sex better for him.

A lot of couples use a vibrator when having sex. It allows the woman to get more aroused and enjoy herself more. Don't be ashamed to introduce it into your sex life. Not every woman can have an orgasm every time she has sex, let alone a vaginal orgasm. The fact of the matter is that most women need clitoral stimulation to reach orgasm.

If you're one of these women and you've never used a vibrator during sex, you're not doing your man any favors by pretending his penis is all you ever need to reach orgasm. Your man wants to see you aroused. It gets him off. Your man wants you to be satisfied and reach orgasm, a real orgasm, every time you have sex.

Besides, the same sex over and over again is going to get old after a while. Using your finger can be drudgery, and it also takes up your entire hand which can be used for other purposes. So, be adventurous and introduce new things into your sex life. The very first thing you should introduce is a vibrator because it's going to increase **your pleasure** in an amazing way. When you're happy, your man's happy.

You don't even have to use a big old dick-shaped vibrator. They have so many different varieties out there to choose from. They have everything from very small and discreet ones, to waterproof ones, to ones that your man can wear! The choices are endless. My personal favorites are the bullets because they're less likely to get in the way and they allow you to be hands-free in certain positions. Another tip to spice things up and make sex funner for you is this stuff called "ON Arousal Oil". You place a few drops on your clitoris a few minutes before sex. It makes sex better and also makes the orgasm stronger.

I always buy my stuff from Adam and Eve because they have the largest selection in the world. They also give out a $10 coupon for new customers when you sign up with your email, and they always have specials and promotions running. They're by far the best sex store out there.

Once you've got your pleasures taken care of, you can venture back onto the site and find endless amounts of fun for you and your man. If you and your man have been together for a long time and you want to put some spunk back into your sex life, this is the perfect place to start. The opportunities for fun and excitement are endless. You can venture on the site together, or you can surprise him with sexy gifts. The site is especially helpful if you live in a small town, that does not provide access to these type of "adventures". Venturing onto Adam and Eve or any online sex store and buying stuff is something that can add a new layer of excitement into your relationship.

Hey, let's be honest. When you've been with someone for years, and even decades, there's nothing wrong with adding spice to your love life. Be honest with one another and be open to trying new things. It can be very healthy for your relationship by helping you grow closer and more intimate with one another.

#3)
Men watch porn.
Men jack off.
It's a fact.

Accept the fact that 95% of men watch porn and jack off behind our backs. Anyone with a dick probably jacks off. It's reality. Accept it. Don't go off on him, call him a pervert, break up, and then throw him and all of his shit out the door just because you catch him watching porn. ***Would you rather him watch porn and jack off or cheat on you?*** Good men stay home and masturbate.

The thing you have to look out for is porn addiction.

There's a big difference between watching occasional pornography and being addicted to it. Addiction can cause a big problem in relationships because it can dull down his senses, provide false expectations, and even go as far as causing impotence aka limp dick.

So, beware of compulsive pornography viewing but excuse the porn sites in his viewing history or porn pop ups. As long as he's being a faithful man, understand that he has needs that are much different and more frequent than yours.

Watching pornography and jacking off is not the same as talking to women on the Internet, exchanging or accepting nude photos, cybersex, or participating in web cam sessions. I think things like that are considered cheating and you know why? If he wouldn't want you doing it, then he shouldn't be doing it. If he caught you watching porn, he probably wouldn't be offended, but if he found pictures of rock hard cocks in your text messages, that would be a whole other story.

So, if you ever run into situations with your man like this, keep in mind that it's normal male behavior to look at pornography and jack off. Don't take it personally. Take it as a sign that he's being faithful to you and would rather jack off than be a cheating man whore. On the other hand, don't tolerate him doing anything that he wouldn't want you doing.

#3)
Try it in different places.

Some of you do this without a second thought. However, for some of you this is going to seem impossible to do. Even some men are completely closed minded to having sex anywhere but in the bedroom. This routine can get to be a problem when you've been with someone for a really long time. You don't have to have sex in different places all the time, but once in a while, give it a try.

It doesn't hurt to occasionally break away from the normal routine, and who knows? You may find it very erotic to have sex in random places. That random place could be as simple as the kitchen table or as outrageous as the public bathroom in the mall. The opportunities are endless. Just don't get caught because you will get arrested.

This can be exciting as well as important to your romance because it can help keep things alive. It also provides you and your man with great memories that last a lifetime. Always remember: Wearing a skirt helps. Be quick about it, and don't get caught. Here are just a few fun ideas that range from simple to just plain illegal:

In the ocean

In a public bathroom

On the beach at night

In a parking lot

In the backyard

Public or State park
(Not a kid's park please, kids play there!)

In your pool or hot tub

On a balcony

In the shower

At work

On a long drive
(Oral sex while driving or pull over at a random spot)

In a forest

Outside in the rain

Airplane bathroom

On a chair

Parked anywhere in your car or truck

At a highway rest stop

On vacation in a random place

In front of the fireplace

In a dressing room

While camping

In a laundry room or on top of your washer/dryer at home

In a box, with a fox

In the rain, on a train

In a house, with a mouse

Just kidding...but as you can see the opportunities are endless.

#4)
Know the difference between
good blow jobs and *great* blow jobs.

Good blow jobs are your regular, run of the mill oral pleasure. These are the ones that you give him on any ordinary day. And if you're thinking, "But I already give my man great blow jobs, and I would never give him average ones." Stop! Hold it right there.

You need to save the mind-blowing great blow jobs for for rewards, negotiations, and positive reinforcement (more about this in the next chapter). Right now, you're simply spoiling him. Spoiling ruins people and makes them unappreciative. Sure, he may appreciate it in the beginning, but what happens when he gets used to them? If you spoil your man with mind blowing oral sex every time, you're robbing yourself of the opportunity to reward him.

This all goes back to pussy power. Don't give up your power so easily, and definitely don't give up your best tricks on a regular basis. For those of you who are uncomfortable with oral sex, or for any woman who would like tips, tricks, and information about how to give the best blow job ever, check out this ebook. It was written by a man, specifically for women.

Always remember blow jobs are only for men you're in a deeply committed relationship with. Save them for that special man that earns them and deserves them. Be smart about when you give them to him and what type you're giving him. Not all blow jobs are created equal. Use the great ones to your advantage and live happily ever after.

#5)
The Best Wedding Present Ever

In this day and age, we rarely wait until marriage to have sex. As unfortunate as that may sound to some, that's reality. Shit, we rarely even wait for marriage to have kids. Our generation is so ass backwards, that a majority of us do the family thing completely out of order. We have kids, eventually get married, and then we buy a house.

Despite our generational dysfunction, there is still one thing you can save for your future husband: entrance through the back door. You may not be able to save him your virginity, but you can save him your virginity of a different variety. Save anal sex for marriage.

When it comes to anal sex there are two types of women. There are the women that claim it's the best sex ever and then there are the women who are like, hell no, get that thing away from there! If you can't even think of doing something like that, then don't. I'm not encouraging anyone to do anything they don't feel comfortable doing. I'm just giving you an idea of how to make your husband feel special, and also an option for spicing things up.

So, for those that would like to offer the man they chose to marry a very special gift, you can save this for your wedding night. You could even skip the wedding night and save it for years down the road when the sex begins to get too regular or mundane. That way you always have that surprise in your back pocket to spice things up.

LOYALTY

Men don't fall in love easily, but when they do it's usually for a lifetime. Take advantage of this fact by remaining loyal and faithful to a man that's truly in love with you. When you do, you will always be happy. You will always have a good man by your side. You will have a loyal partner for a lifetime. Someone to grow old with. Someone to wipe away your tears. You will be in one of those relationships that some women only dream about.

Don't ever allow a foolish mistake to ruin such a beautiful thing.

Sometimes when we've been with someone for a really long time, we get too comfortable. When we get too comfortable, we begin to get bored. When a person begins to get bored, they may fall into the trap of thinking there's someone better out there. They may begin to foolishly believe that the single life seems more appealing; naively forgetting the downsides of it after years or decades of being in a commitment.

There's something I've always said, "The single life is fun and lonely, and the married life brings happiness and boredom." Each has its ups and downs. That's why it's important to enjoy the single life when you're young and save marriage and long term commitments for later. However, once you're deeply committed or married, you should *never* allow the boredom to override your happiness.

Don't ever fall into believing that the grass is greener on the other side. This is a mistake both men and women can easily make within a marriage. Unfortunately for the ones that make it, it's usually a decision they come to deeply regret later on, but only after it's too late to recover their marriage and they've come to realize that the grass was not greener. It was actually dead and covered in cow shit.

So, be forewarned about the green grass scam. If you're married or in a long term committed relationship with a good man, there may come a time when another man comes into your world and tries to trick you. He may try to deceive you with feelings of excitement. He may confuse you by turning you on in a way that you haven't felt in a while. He may con you into believing that you deserve better. However, be warned. Don't be the fool.

Never ever fall in love with a stranger.

Don't allow some new guy to walk into your life and steal you away from your good man. A lot of times when men try to steal another man's woman, it's for the same stupid reasons that women do this to other women. It's all for the fun, excitement, and ego high. **Be wary of any man that tries to lure you away from a loyal mate**. A lot of men do this purely for the sex, but some have more sinister agendas and these are the men that do it for the thrill of stealing another man's woman.

When it's all said and done, and he's had you bent over in every way possible or he's convinced you to completely overhaul your entire life to be with him, that's when his true colors will show. There are a few things that may happen at this point: Once he has sabotaged your relationship, the fun for him may be over and he may move on. He may lose interest in you sexually and move on to his next victim. Or, he may enter into a long term relationship with you and that's when you end up realizing he's a piece of shit. (Because what kind of man does this kind of stuff? *A man lacking integrity.*)

Or, you may just live happily ever after. The chances of the latter happening are very, very low. The chances that you will end up regretting your decision and being the one that suffers in the end are very, very high. Don't be the victim. Never allow another man to come in between you and your good man. Not for some butterflies in your tummy. Not for some temporary excitement. And especially not for some dick. It's just not worth it.

If you ever find yourself in this situation, rather than turn to a stranger, turn to your man. Be honest about the way you feel. Talk openly about any problems you may have. If you need him to be more spontaneous, just say it. I'm 100% sure he would prefer you talk to him and be honest, than to have an affair or leave him for another man. Show him the same respect that you would expect to receive if the shoe was on the other foot.

Loyalty is what a true marriage is all about. A loyal man is hard to find these days, so when you find him, you return the favor by remaining just as loyal to him. Loyalty is just as important to men as it is to us. More importantly, loyalty is the foundation of a love that stands the test of time.

Be dedicated. Be loyal. Remain faithful, through the good times and the bad times, through the fun times and the boring times. Expect the same from him. If this man is just as loyal and dedicated to you, you will both have the privilege of enjoying an amazing romance. A romance that some people will only experience through reading a romance novel. You will have a relationship that no other man or woman could ever come between. A beautiful and meaningful relationship that will lead to a lifelong unbreakable bond.

Chapter Six

The Power of the Married Pussy

In the first book I covered using PEAK, PES and Pussy Power for single women, and women trying to gain the love, respect, and the commitment they desired from the men in their lives. Well, married woman have a lot of power too. It's only fair that I dedicate a chapter to the power of the married pussy.

Teaching an Old Dog New Tricks

They say you can't teach an old dog new tricks, but with the power of pussy, there's nothing you can't do! If your relationship is one in which your husband has the upper hand and you want to learn how to use pussy power to gain some level playing ground, this is the chapter for you. If your relationship is one where the passion has faded over the years, or your man's treatment of you has gradually decreased over the years, this chapter is for you.

I get a ton of emails from women asking how they can use The Power of the Pussy on their husbands to elicit a change. Now, I'm not going to lie to you, it's not easy to change the dynamic of a relationship once it's been established, but where there's a will, there's a way. And if there's one way it can be done, it's with the amazingly hypnotic power of being a woman.

Married women can use their power for a variety of issues. No matter what the issue is in your relationship, whether it's getting him to be nicer, more helpful, or more romantic, you have the power to make him change. Even women who feel their marriages are headed for divorce can find help within these pages. You may feel powerless now, but by the time you're done with this section you will feel refreshed and ready to tackle a variety of marital problems.

The Five "P's"

Anything you want to get a married man to do can be accomplished by using the five P's to your advantage.

#1) PEAK (Pre-Ejaculation Ass Kissing)
#2) PES (Post Ejaculation Syndrome)
#3) Patience and Persistence
#4) Positive Reinforcement
#5) Pussy Negotiations

I'm going to cover how to use each of these in this chapter. I want to do a quick review of PEAK, PES, and "Just Say It" for those who haven't read the first book, or if it's been awhile. If you've read the first book, I apologize for repeating this information. However, I think it's a good idea to review this information because it's the foundation of using pussy power, especially within a marriage. So, here we go...

PEAK: PEAK is Pre-Ejaculation Ass Kissing. PEAK is when it's been a few hours/days/weeks since he has had sex. The exact time frame depends on your man's sexual appetite. PEAK is the time between when he wants to get some and when you actually give him some. It's the most important time frame for utilizing pussy power. It's an imperative time frame that must be acknowledged, appreciated, and respected by you because it's your greatest tool when dealing with men.

Men, whether married or not, are always more willing to be nice, sweet, agreeable, romantic, and willing to negotiate during PEAK. Testosterone is building up inside of his balls, just dying to get out. To put it bluntly, PEAK is the time frame leading up to when he's the most horny and craving sexual stimulation. PEAK is when we have the most power!

PES: PES is PEAK's evil opposite. PES is Post Ejaculation Syndrome. PES is when pussy power is at its weakest. PES is the attitude change they get after they have sex. He probably doesn't even realize his attitude changes, and perhaps you never have either. It's a very slight change, but it makes a huge difference in their level of kindness and cooperation.

From now on, start paying attention to the way he acts during the time frame leading up to sex compared to the time frame shortly after sex. You will begin to see the slight shift and difference in his attitude. Once you begin to notice the slight changes in his personality, you can use this knowledge to your advantage.

Notice how during PES he will be less willing to bend or compromise with you. He will be a lot less willing to kiss your ass, and he will probably be a lot cockier than normal. Once a man busts a nut, he is no longer in "need" of you anymore. I know that sounds *so* wrong, but when you're aware of it, you can do something about it, rather than just being pissed off and angry that he's being an asshole. Being angry is not empowering. Being aware and using this knowledge to your advantage is where the power lies!

Hey, it's going to happen whether we like it or not. Men are sexual beings. They are motivated by pussy. It's only natural that after they have sex, they will no longer have the same level of motivation to be nice, sweet, charming, and helpful. He's satisfied. For the time being...

The good news is that PES doesn't last that long. Depending on your man's sexual appetite, it could last a few hours up to a few days. The bad news is that during this time frame you've lost a lot of your pussy power over him. It's hard for us to get much of what we want or need out of a man, especially right after PES. You want the garbage taken out? He responds with a little attitude, "Yeah, I'll get to it." You want your back massaged? He brushes you off with, "I'm tired". We've all noticed how men like to pass out right after sex and couldn't care less if it makes us mad? That's PES.

You're swimming upstream when trying to get anything from a man during PES, so don't even bother. This is when fights are easily started because he's being an asshole and you don't understand why. Well, now you know why... it's PES! If you need something from him during this time, whether it's love and attention or a light bulb changed, but he's in PES mode... you're most likely going to encounter resistance or an uncaring attitude. Then you get angry and frustrated and it creates a bad cycle.

Avoid fights and frustrations by paying attention to how your man acts after sex and how long after sex before he returns to PEAK and starts being "himself" again. As I mentioned earlier PES may last a few hours, a few days, or for the less sexually active men, it may even last a week or two. It all depends on your man's sexual needs and how often he likes to have sex. Study your man's behavior and time frames because each man is unique.

I know for my man his PES usually lasts a day...two at the most. He is too damn horny to go too long without it. Usually the day of and the day after we have sex, I notice the PES attitude change. It's not a huge shift, but it's enough of a difference for me to think to myself, "Okay, no problem. Be an asshole now, because you'll be back to wanting something from me in no time." And sure enough by the next day he is beginning to make a turn back into the sweet guy I fell in love with.

I like to wait a few days to let it really build up and give him something to appreciate when it's time to make sweet love again. (Well, there's that and the fact that we have three kids, so time and privacy is hard to come by.) By the time PEAK rolls back around again, he's cooking dinner, rubbing my back, kissing my neck, and telling me how much he loves me.

Sure, a good man will do these things all of the time, without the need of using pussy power tactics... in a perfect world. Don't get me wrong, my man probably would too... with constant reminders, bitching, resentment, and resistance. However, using PEAK to my advantage, it all gets done happily and with a smile, rather than with hesitation, procrastination, or an attitude.

Pussy power wielded skillfully simply makes life easier. No fighting needs to take place to remind him to help out. All I have to do is wait for PES to pass and then ask him to do things when he's in PEAK mode. The good news for us is that when it comes to men, that's a vast majority of the time!

Now that we've gone over PEAK and PES, an important part of utilizing PEAK and PES is "Just Say It".

Just Say It: "Just Say It" means speaking up and directly asking for what you want in a sweet and sexy way during PEAK. It's best used for those conversations or topics you want to discuss about your relationship, but you just can't seem to get his attention or perhaps you feel uncomfortable bringing it up. It serves to give you the strength and support you need to bring up certain topics about the relationship. "Just Say It" and PEAK work together to get his attention. Below are some important tips to remember when using PEAK and "Just Say It."

Stop Assuming: One thing you need to remember about using PEAK and "Just Say It" is to stop assuming. You're going to have to plainly ask for what you want instead of *assuming he knows*. Men are not like us. We're naturally more intuitive and attentive. We notice a lot of little details and we can easily pick up when something's off, so I guess we assume that they're the same way too. The reality is that most men don't pay nearly as much attention to these kinds of things like we do.

Sure, in a perfect world we would like to believe that men are intuitive with our needs and are concerned enough to know when something's wrong, but that's not the reality of a man's thought process. They can really be clueless sometimes! Especially when it comes to our emotions, wants, and needs. It takes a lot of door slamming, teeth sucking, hint-dropping, and huffing and puffing before they begin to notice there's an issue. Then we expect them to guess or to automatically know what's wrong. Then we get mad when they don't! These poor guys, we really give them a run for their money sometimes.

Do yourself a favor by never expecting or assuming that a man knows what's on your mind. You must speak up. Men are not psychic. They cannot read our minds. Speak your mind openly and honestly about issues and always do it during PEAK. Using "Just Say It" during PEAK will allow you to get to a resolution before it even becomes a problem. Let him know what he does that makes you upset. Let him know what makes you happy. Let's avoid drama and go straight for the kill by using PEAK and "Just Say It" to our advantage.

K.I.S.S. (Keep It Simple Stupid): Another very important thing to remember about using "Just Say It" is that you only want to talk about one issue at a time. Men have one-track minds. If you go off topic or go on a tangent about several things at once, you're only hurting your chances of getting what you desire. PEAK and "Just Say It" are not to be used as an hour-long counseling session. You don't want to overload him or bombard him with so many problems or topics that he gets overwhelmed and frustrated.

Remember, men don't think like us. Ever notice how well we can multitask, but they prefer to focus on one thing at a time? It's the way their brains are wired. It's a scientific fact that men are good at focusing and we're the queens of multitasking. Most of them can only process and correct one problem at a time. Once the issue is resolved (and this may take a few rounds of PEAK) then you can move on to the next issue in your relationship.

K.I.S.A.S. (Keep it Sweet and Sexy): When it comes to communicating with men, being sweet and sexy during PEAK will be the easiest way to get his attention and get him to act on your request and change his behavior. Simply because you plainly and directly asked him. They respond so much better to this style of communication. The sweet and sexy tone is imperative. Nagging gets tuned out. Bitching makes them resistant. Sweet, sexy, and simple is speaking on their wave length. They will tune you in, instead of tuning you out.

Why Your Power May Have Been Disconnected

The reason some women have a hard time using pussy power on their man is because they're going about it backwards. The simple yet vital mistake women make in their relationships that allows the man all of the control is getting these PEAK and PES techniques backwards. This usually happens for two reasons, allow me to explain.

Either they started the relationship off by giving their man great sex whenever he wanted it. This usually leads to the man being spoiled and/or entitled and the woman being powerless, and unfortunately for the woman, it remains that way throughout the relationship. Or, she mistakenly thought that he would be nicer if she gave him good sex all of the time. In this scenario the relationship may have started off with power, but the dynamic flipped at some point or slowly changed over time due to the mistake of using pussy power backwards.

The problem with either of these situations is that it's the completely wrong way to use pussy power. Logically, it seems that this style would yield results. However, this only spoils them and makes them unappreciative of your wonderful gift. So, if you're having issues with your man, whatever they may be, switch things around.

Stop *spoiling him* with good pussy on demand.
Start *rewarding him* with good pussy for good behavior.

Patience and Persistence

Women in these situations will have to shift and mold the

power back to their favor. This is no easy task, but it can be done. This is where the patience and persistence comes in. Expect some hostility in the beginning if he's not used to being told no. Things aren't going to change immediately.

Remember, if you've spoiled him, he is used to things the way they are. He likes things the way they are. It's easier for him. He's going to resist change. He may even throw temper tantrums or hissy-fits at the thought of not getting what he wants when he wants it.

It's similar to trying to change the behavior of a spoiled kid. You have to break the bad habit of giving in to their every whim at some point. The day you do there's going to be resistance, it's going to be difficult at first. However, with persistence and patience things will slowly begin to change.

Whenever you're having a hard day because he's being an asshole, just remind yourself that change isn't easy. Be patient. It won't be easy for you and it won't be easy for him. Remember, he's not used to this style of interacting with you. However, work diligently for a few weeks or months at getting things switched around and you will be amazed at how much easier life will be for the both of you.

What to do if You Encounter Resistance

During the difficult days remember that PES doesn't last forever. So, let him have his little cocky attitude change because the joke's on him. PEAK will roll right back around and you will be back in control! Make him wait a tiny bit longer than you normally would to feel the full effects of PEAK. Want him to be more romantic? Now is the time to ask. Want him to help with the kids more? Now is the time to ask. Whatever it is that you seek from him, PEAK is the time in which to ask.

You have to do this subliminally. No one has to know you're trying to change things around, especially not him. Now, if you're dealing with the type of guy that's hard headed, or perhaps he's used to you being submissive, you may have to turn the PEAK up a notch and add even more bang for your buck. Try these tips when using PEAK, PES, and "Just Say It." Especially if you're encountering resistance.

Positive Reinforcement

In psychology, positive reinforcement is defined as a reward that's given for a specific desired behavior. Other behaviors, especially those that are negative, are simply ignored. Over time, this will lead to an increase in the desired behavior.

Using pussy power during PEAK and not allowing sex or sexual stimulation during PES is positive reinforcement at its finest. When he's in a good mood and/or being good to you and treating you in a way that makes you happy, make a note to yourself to give him a nice surprise that evening. Make it something special, like a passionate blow job or a session of sex that leaves his mind blown. Whatever type of sexual desires you know he wants, but you wouldn't normally do, is what you want to use as your reinforcement. **The bigger and better his behavioral change was, the bigger and better the reward should be.**

To make your positive reinforcement even more effective say something about his good behavior and relate it to the sexual reward. For example, while beginning to do your sexual reward or before doing it say something like, "The way you treated me today... makes me wanna suck your dick!" and then give him a good quality blow job. I know it sounds funny, but I'm serious. This will link the good behavior to the sexual activity in his mind and that's exactly what you want to happen.

This is letting him know that good behavior gets him

rewards (and GOOD rewards, not the boring same ole' same ole' sex.) Always reward good behavior with positivity rather than scolding bad behavior with fighting, rude comments, or the silent treatment. For men, sex and sexually related behavior is about as positive as it can get.

So, to all my married women, you CAN teach an old dog new tricks. When your dog does what you want him to do, give him treats. When he's being bad, you ignore his bad behavior and you certainly don't give him any treats.

On those PES days when he's being an asshole, don't give him any sexual attention at all. Regularly allowing sex or sexual activity rather than ignoring the bad behavior is a huge mistake. Unfortunately this has taught him that whether or not he's an asshole, he gets what he wants.

There's no incentive for being a kind and sweet guy. Ignore bad behavior and reward good behavior. Technically you're not even ignoring bad behavior. He doesn't know it, but he's being punished for his bad behavior by not getting sex or sexual favors during his PES faze.

Another important thing to remember is that positive reinforcement must be individualized to the specific person receiving it. What reinforces one person's behavior may not have the same effect on someone else. You know your man best, so only you know what will have the greatest affect. You know what makes him smile and gets him excited.

Explore and discover what motivates your man. Vary the rewards to keep him engaged. Men don't only respond to sex. They could also want food, praise, or attention. Stroke his ego. Compliment him. Try a strip tease. Cook a nice dinner in the nude and serve it to him naked and then initiate sex on the kitchen table. Clean naked. Perform oral sex in the car while he's driving. Be creative and give rewards based on what you think would make your man jump for joy.

Do something you normally wouldn't do. Get out of your comfort zone. When we've been with someone for many years, or even decades, we tend to get stuck in a rut. Allow your rewards to be something outside of the rut. Get creative, get freaky, and don't be afraid to be naughty. This is your husband. If there's anyone or anytime for you to be a nasty girl, it's with him, within your marriage, and for the purpose of positive change.

Pussy Negotiations

Pussy negotiations are fun and quite possibly my favorite part about being a girl! Pussy negotiations are when you motivate your man to do things for you or to get things that you want. It's actually pussy power in action. During PEAK moments, think to yourself, "What good can come of this round of sex? Should I ask him to bathe the kids and put them to bed? Should I ask him to do the dishes, cook dinner, or wash laundry?"

I like to let PEAK build up a few days, right down to the last minute, when he just can't take it anymore. That's the best time to enter into negotiations. I love massages, and to be honest, that's usually what I want. Sometimes I will ask for a variety of things and 99.9% of the time I will get it all.

People will say it's wrong or call it manipulation. Call it what you want, but I'm happy and my man's happy and that's all that matters. A lot of couples, especially ones who have been together for a really long time, work through these negotiations. He gets his needs met, and she gets her needs met. There's nothing wrong with that!

When it comes to pussy negotiations, and getting your man to do specific tasks, you have to go back to the basics of "Just Say It." Be brave. Don't be afraid to ask. Be sexy. Be sweet. Be reasonable.

If you're close to your husband you may be able to be blunt about it. For example, you could simply say, "Babe, let's make a deal. If you bathe the kids, get them into bed, and rub my back for a little while, I will (insert sexy statement that you know will spark his interest.)"

Another important thing to remember is to make sure you get him to do all of the stuff before sex or it could be an issue if you wait until after sex. I'm still waiting for a back massage I negotiated back in 2005. It was the one time I said, "Okay, you can do it later." I will never make that mistake again.

So, pussy negotiations are good for little everyday things and positive reinforcement is used more for bigger issues that require lasting change. When all else fails and all of the above tactics don't work, then you've got some pretty hefty issues to work through. If this is the case for you then it may be time to go to war...

Going to War

Always try "Just Say It," positive reinforcement, and negotiations first. Be patient and be persistent. However, if you feel that you've done everything you possibly could and he's just not budging, you may have to take it to the next level. You may need to go to war by using negative reinforcement and mind games. Yes, I know, mind games are so wrong. Whatever. Drastic times call for drastic measures.

If your man does not respond to multiple attempts at positive reinforcement, then you either married an asshole that's never going to change, or you have a man that's an asshole so much of the time you never have a reason to reward him. In either case, you may have to take very drastic measures to elicit change.

Be prepared. This way is not easy. This way is a gamble and therefore is ONLY to be used in cases where the next step would be separation or divorce. You're going to get one of two results with this method. Either he's going to change and your relationship will change for the better OR you're going to break up. Don't attempt this unless you're prepared to separate if things don't change. The reward of winning will be worth the gamble, *especially* if you know in your heart that things are going to lead to a divorce soon.

You're going to have to make a BIG change in yourself for a significant period of time. You're going to try playing his own games on him. Treat him the way he treats you. If he walks around with an attitude and ignores you, do the same to him. Stop catering to him. Stop walking around on those eggshells. Begin to act like you don't care. ***Act the way you would act if you were having an affair, very aloof and uninterested.***

Do this for a few days or a few weeks and see what happens. The reason you're going to try this is because it's human nature to want people more when they don't want us. When they won't give us attention, we want the attention more. Perhaps you've been so good to him that he doesn't appreciate your love and attention, so take it away from him for a while. You may be able to get his attention by doing this. When he asks you what your problem is the first few times, don't crack. Blow him off and keep it up.

When he finally breaks down and has had enough of it, that's when you're going to calmly ask him to sit down and talk. Say it in gentle but firm tone, "We need to talk. It's important." At this point he's probably scared you're going to tell him that you're having an affair, or you're filing for divorce. In reality, you're just gearing him up to tell him the truth.

That's where the mind games come in. You've subliminally tricked him into thinking he's going to lose you. You've got his attention now (and you've probably got him a little bit scared too). This is when you're going to ask for what you need. Let him know that you're sick of not feeling loved or appreciated, that you're sick of walking around unhappy (or whatever the big issue in the relationship is). Tell him you're tired of it and you want a change.

He's either going to try to change or he's not. Either way you have your answer as to your next step. Sometimes marriages get off track. If you can't get your marriage back on track, then don't be afraid to take the next step. Separation or divorce. You cannot live the remainder of your life in an unhappy marriage. If he will not change and you decide to stay and stick it out then you have no one to blame but yourself for your unhappiness. But, at least you can say you tried your hardest.

The one time when it will be hardest to get either positive or negative reinforcements to work is if he's having an affair. If he has someone on the side, he has someone to run to and an excuse to leave and blame it all on you. So, be careful. But, if you have the balls, you can call his bluff. When he threatens to leave, tell him to go. Tell him you're not going to live under the constant uncertainty of his threats.

Let him know that you can find a new man. Be confident in your ability to be a single woman. If he tries to put you down and say rude things, like "no man will want you" and other nonsense, don't fall for it. And certainly don't let him see you believing those lies! There's so many men out there, I don't care how old you are, how over weight you are, how financially ruined you may become, there's always other men to turn to.

Know in your heart that you will find a better man, and allow the confidence in that fact to show through. That confidence and belief will send a very strong message to him. A message he knows deep down inside but would never admit to you.

He knows there are plenty of men out there that would have you as their wife, but he will never admit that fact to you because it's too empowering. You must be firm and unafraid. Tell him you're not afraid to be alone and you're not afraid to start over again. You're tired of being treated badly when there's plenty of men out there that would be good to you.

He has to know that you're not afraid of him leaving, because when they know you depend on them—whether financially, emotionally, or both—they know they have the upper hand. **An asshole will use that upper hand to his advantage every time.**

It's an unfortunate fact that this sometimes happens to us when we're the stay at home mom or financially dependent on our man. It can lead to a very fucked up situation if control is placed into the wrong hands. We can get stuck because we depend on them, and if they want to be assholes and use our dependency against us, they can.

What if He Cheats?

Well, then what the hell are you doing staying married to a man that cheats!? I don't think any person should tolerate disrespect like that. If a person is cheating on you, then I think you should leave that person. However, I know that sometimes it's not that easy. So, let's put that obvious solution to the side and explore this topic.

I believe that pussy power will still work on the cheating man IF he's cheating on you for either of the following reasons. Do you think he's cheating because over the years you've begun to hate having sex with him? Have you become bored with the sex and therefore don't want it anymore? Have you stopped having sex with him? **Be honest.** If the answers to any of those questions are yes, that's good news. You can fix this problem.

Let's be real here. When people have been together for a really long time, sometimes the sex gets boring. It's the same old thing over and over and over again. Plus, as women we can sometimes get overloaded with all of our daily duties and just be too tired to even think about sex. Then add in the fact that you have kids running around or sleeping in the next room and it feels impossible to get relaxed enough to get into the mood. Men don't get it, but sometimes it's just too difficult to relax enough to enjoy sex.

Add all of these factors together and combine it with the fact that our sex drive can die out with hormonal imbalances, and we can easily slip into a mindset of being completely uninterested in sex. Sometimes we just don't want sex the way we did when the relationship was new and exciting. So, perhaps you've been pushing your man's sexual advances away for too long. Or, perhaps you've been lying there staring at the ceiling, telling him to hurry up one too many times. If this goes on year after year, some men are just going to look for sex elsewhere. Horny bastards.

It's the sad truth. Remember, men are sexual by nature, just as we are emotional by nature. If a man doesn't satisfy our emotional needs, we will grow tired of that and seek emotional stability from someone else. Men are similar when it comes to sex. And no, I don't believe that *all* men cheat. I do believe that if you neglect your husband's sexual needs for long enough that eventually he *might* cheat.

This is not to excuse a cheating man's bad behavior. It only serves to recognize if you have a hand in the problem, because if you do, then you can fix it. So, it's good news and bad news. Of course, no one wants to be cheated on, but if his cheating is due to your lack of interest in him sexually, then the good news is that the situation can be fixed.

If you really love your man... if you don't want your marriage to end due to infidelity... if you think you can accept some responsibility... and you think you can forgive him, then make it your goal to use the techniques in this chapter and throughout both books to spice up your relationship. It's in these situations that pussy power can bring that roaming dog home.

However, if a man's cheating on you and there's an

emotional tie to the woman he's having the affair with, this is going to add a whole new level of difficulty to the situation. You can first try the tactics mentioned above to try and reel him back home, but if it doesn't work or if your husband has admitted that he loves this other woman, you should consider leaving. The only way he's going to wake up out of his fantasy is to give him a reality check. Continuing to have sex with him or continuing the relationship as it once was is only serving his needs and desires.

If he has two women fighting over him, that's stroking his ego. Don't serve to stroke his ego any more. You must leave. If a man tells you he no longer loves you anymore, then you know there's no repairing the damage. Don't continue to torture yourself by trying to make things work. Let him have his whore and in time he will see the error of his ways. Unfortunately, they usually don't realize their mistakes until it's too late and you've officially moved on. Sitting around torturing yourself serves no purpose. You must be strong and move on.

Now, if you have a man that's cheating because he has an insatiable appetite for sex that no woman can fulfill, then you just have a problem on your hands. There's nothing you can do to tame a wild man that has no intentions of being faithful.

In either of the last two scenarios, nothing's going to change him... except losing you for good. In either case you will never know until you walk away and leave him for good. He has to know that you're gone and officially moved on before you will see him come crawling back begging for forgiveness and willing to be faithful to you. If that doesn't work, then there's nothing you can do but move on, be single, and eventually find a new man that has values and integrity. Well, you can always stay with him and put up with that cheating crap, but you know and I know that you don't deserve that.

Should I Take Him Back?

If you're separated from your husband for whatever reason, whether it's due to the issues mentioned above or you were separated before you ever picked up this book, you may be wondering if and when you should take him back. Taking a man back should always be based on two things. The first being his efforts and sincerity in trying to win you back. The second being your ability to forgive him.

People make mistakes... and sometimes they need to make mistakes to learn hard lessons. Sometimes a man has to lose his woman to realize what he had. If he's determined to win your heart back, make him work for it. Make him prove to you that he's serious by making him put in effort. Watch his actions. Don't just let him talk about what he's going to do differently. Tell him he needs to prove it through actions, not words.

This takes time. Let him beg and work at winning you over until YOU feel he deserves to have the relationship back. This is not up to him. Do not allow him to rush you or pressure you into making a decision before you're ready. You can even make him beg until you feel he's just about to give up, until he feels all hope is lost. Then... BAM!!!

Forgive him and work it out.

Always let it be known before you seal the deal, that this will be the last time you ever forgive him. You will NOT tolerate cheating, lying, disrespect (or whatever issues caused the separation). You only desire an honest and faithful man, and anything less is below your standards.

Now, if you decide to get back with him, you have some work to do as well. Can you put this behind you? Forgiveness is very important. You can't try to move forward with tons of resentment and anger. You need to be 100% sure that you can forgive him. You also need to be able to tell him you've forgiven him once you've reconciled.

If he's being honest about his fuck up, and his desire to work things out and change is real, and he truly loves you, your forgiveness will feel like a ton of bricks being lifted off his shoulders. Your forgiveness is essential. It's one of the stepping stones that will lead to a reconciliation that's meaningful and lasting.

**When all else fails...
divorce that mother fucker!**

Chapter Seven

The Power of the Divorced Pussy

This chapter is going to address the various complexities of divorce. More importantly it's going to help you overcome these complexities in a positive way that enables you to move through this rough time in your life with a smile on your face. This chapter may very well help you keep your sanity during the toughest and darkest days of divorce. Whether you're currently contemplating a divorce, you're a woman in the middle of dealing with a divorce, and especially if you're a woman who's having a difficult time getting over your divorce, this chapter is for you.

Even if you're a women who wasn't married, but you're going through a bad break up with a man you've been with for a very long time, lived together, or had children together, for emotional purposes and for the purposes of this chapter, I want you to consider yourself divorced or going through a divorce. When you've lived with someone for years, and especially if you have children involved, it's a common-law marriage and any separation or breakup can be considered a divorce all the same.

In our day and age, we tend to stray away from marriage. I suspect it's because too many of us have come from divorced families, or have witnessed too many marriages fail and end in divorce. Therefore we've become an entire generation traumatized by the word marriage. For some of us, it's almost as if getting married is an automatic jinx for failure. So, we prefer to avoid the drama of a legal marriage. Instead, we opt into long-term committed relationships, have children, and live together. So, when I refer to the word divorce, apply it to a break-up if you feel the intensity of your situation is equivalent to a divorce.

When it comes to divorce, women usually fall into one of three categories. In one of these categories are the women who are currently contemplating divorce but not sure if they should go ahead with it. If this is your situation, I highly suggest you read the chapter titled, "The Power of the Baby Daddy." This chapter contains seven very important questions and an exercise that will help you to look at your situation objectively and make a wise decision. You should combine the information from that chapter with the exercises and advice from the first book to help you make a clear and wise decision.

The other two categories involve women who are currently in the middle of a divorce or women who are recently divorced. Within these categories, you could be dealing with a variety of emotions. You could be a woman that is happily making the choice to divorce and therefore feel empowered and excited about your decision.

Or, you could be on the other end of the spectrum, and dealing with a divorce that's leaving you emotionally drained and completely devastated. You may even fall somewhere in between, bouncing around between emotions of being happy and sad, relieved and distraught, or courageous and scared, all at the same time.

Divorce is complex. It's not easy. You're literally taking one life and splitting into two. There are going to be some growing pains with a change that drastic. Just the thought of all the things that need to get done can be overwhelming. Then add the emotional roller coaster on top of all the life-changing details, and one can feel like they're on the verge of a nervous breakdown.

If you're a woman who's getting divorced by choice, the situation may not be as painful, but even being the one to initiate and want the divorce is still tough and hard to go through. This is especially true for women, because we can easily make ourselves feel very guilty about our decisions. Even if we know with 100% certainty that we're making the right choice, the guilt of that choice is still lingering in our conscience. However, if this is your scenario, be thankful, because it's much easier than the alternative...

The hardest and most difficult scenario would have to be the woman who recently went through or is currently dealing with a devastating divorce which was not by her choice. The woman who was blindsided and left behind by someone she loved. Whether it's because of infidelity, love lost, or some other issue, this type of divorce can be very traumatic and leave a lasting impression on the soul.

The good news is that there's power in divorce! However, you've got to get past the pain in order to get to the other side to discover that power. Here's how to get there...

Positive Perspective

In the midst of all the pain and devastation of divorce, there's a light at the end of the tunnel. Positive perspective is that light. However, it's up to you to find that light. That's what this chapter is going help you with, step by step. You should take the advice offered in this chapter very seriously if you truly want to heal from divorce and come out of it more empowered.

Commit yourself to following the steps, so that you can find that light. When you do, a whole new world awaits you. A world filled with happiness, fun, and excitement. There is life after divorce. You will get through this and you will be a happier person once it's all over.

Besides, the only other alternative to escaping the pain is to wait it out. Who has time for that? Time heals all wounds, but a positive perspective will get you through all of this much, much faster. Let's speed up the healing process, so we can get you to all that your new life has to offer. Let's find your specific positive perspective so that you can turn the page and enter into the next chapter of your life.

The Five Steps of Positive Perspective

Gaining a positive perspective takes work. It's not an easy task. There are five steps to gaining a positive perspective. The steps are listed below and each will be covered in the following sections.

1) **Grieving Time**
2) **The Deadline**
3) **The Ceremony**
4) **Purposeful Thinking**
5) **Celebration**

Grieving Time

Before you can begin to change your perspective, you need to acknowledge and feel your pain. You need to allow yourself time to grieve. It's okay to be distraught, sad, and paralyzed by the emotions of divorce. You need to give yourself a few weeks, up to a few months, of personal grieving time. You need to purge your emotions.

One of the ways you can purge is by asking yourself a few questions to gain some insight into your feelings. Try to pinpoint exactly what is making you cry. Are you afraid of being alone? Are you scared to let go of the years you've invested? Are you sad about splitting your family up? Did you truly love him and so you feel like you're mourning his loss? Is it all or a combination of these things?

Explore the details of your sadness and write it all down. Get it all out on paper, so that it's out of your head. Feel the feelings. Cry. Let it all out...

Don't fall into the trap of seeing all the great aspects of the relationship and forget all of the negative stuff. Sometimes when we're heartbroken, we only remember the good times. We tend to forget about all the bad times, bad behaviors, and irritating qualities. Grieve and acknowledge your pain, but don't allow your pain to put you into a mindset of denial about the relationship. This is a great time to create your "Things I Hate About You List" from book one (if you haven't already). This list will remind you of the down sides of the relationship, and keep you from dwelling on all that you've lost.

Accept your pain as valid. Whatever your fears are, or for whatever reason you're sad, you have a right to feel the way you do. After your divorce you should allow yourself time to cry and mourn the loss of your marriage. Cry all day in the beginning if you need to. Get the emotions and the tears out of your system. Do not keep them bottled up inside.

However, after a few weeks, up to a few months, you need to begin to limit yourself to one hour of crying per day. This is where the power of controlling your emotions comes in and you will need to do some tough emotional work. You can choose to ignore this advice and feel that you need lots and lots of time to work through all of this pain, and that's fine. Just be warned that you're only lengthening your healing time.

Why drag out the pain? Why do that to yourself? Haven't you been through enough? Why torture yourself by allowing yourself to sit and dwell on negative feelings of sadness and despair for months on end? You're a beautiful woman that deserves to be happy. No one can get you past this divorce but you. Not me, not another book, not your ex, not your girlfriends, nothing and no one can heal you and get you past this divorce but yourself and Father Time.

The Deadline

The next thing you do is set a deadline. The deadline of despair. When you reach this deadline you will no longer feel sorry for yourself. You will no longer be allowed to focus on the negative. On the days leading up to your deadline prepare yourself to toughen up. You've allowed yourself to feel the pain, to cry, and to purge emotion, now you must allow yourself to heal.

There are three reasons why you must get to the point of controlling the tears and emotions. First off, wallowing in negativity is similar to torturing yourself. Crying and mourning in the beginning is acceptable, even healthy, but torturing yourself for months on end will not fix anything. Besides, your ex has tormented you long enough. Don't punish yourself any further.

Secondly, the longer you cry and mourn, the longer you're keeping yourself from moving forward with your life. You have no idea what's waiting for you on the other side of life. Don't spend too much time crying, because while you're collecting tears, you may be missing out on something wonderful.

Lastly and more importantly, try to remember that every day you're sad is one less day of your life that you're happy. So, allow yourself to cry, but set a day on your calendar. This is your negativity deadline. All self-pity ceases on this day and from this day forward you will actively work at controlling your emotions.

When this day comes, go back to book one, chapter one, and be prepared to follow the advice. Controlling your emotions is not easy. It's going to take some tough emotional work, but it must be accomplished. It's the women that do this work that will heal from their divorces and move onto bigger and better things in a relatively short amount of time.

The ones that don't work through the emotional baggage will simply draw out the painful experience for months or even years. Who wants to linger in pain like that? So, do the work and heal, so you can begin to move on to your new life! This is going to be exciting! There's nothing to fear because everything happens for a reason.

When God closes one door, he opens another. But, you

have to be willing to walk away from the closed door and walk through the open door to discover what's in store for you. Go into this life change with a positive attitude, no matter how depressed you may be over the situation. The next step to kicking off your new life with a positive perspective is by having a small and personal ceremony.

The Fuck You Ceremony

On the day that the deadline comes I want you to have a fuck you ceremony. This is when you officially say fuck you to your ex and you mark the special occasion with a symbolic ceremony. The ceremony doesn't have to be anything big. This is just a symbolic event that's going to mark the beginning of your new life and allow you to ceremoniously "let go."

You can accomplish this in a variety of ways. You can burn his pictures, throw your ring into the ocean, or better yet, sell your ring and spend the money on something special for yourself. Put his picture on the wall and throw darts at his face. Do anything and everything that makes you feel refreshed or allows you to release some anger.

This is the perfect time to take out your "Things I Hate About You" list from book one and hang it around the house along with some of his ugliest pictures. Every time you walk by the list and picture, say "fuck you, loser!" or whatever statement allows you to vent.

The opportunities to ceremoniously mark your new life and let go of your old life are endless and will be different for each woman. Do something outrageous. Do something you've thought about doing, but felt too guilty or scared to do, like bleaching his best shirts or breaking his favorite tool. Of course, you never have admit that you did it! You can always play stupid or claim it was an accident if he confronts you.

Please don't feel bad about this, especially if your man left you in a hurtful, deceptive, or devastating way. Consider it a cheaper alternative to therapy. This freedom ceremony is about two things. It's about you getting some of your anger and frustration out, but it's also about doing something symbolic to represent the end of your old life and the beginning of your new life.

Be creative and find a way to celebrate your new life that makes you feel good and allows you to release pent up anger. For some women the guilt of breaking and ruining things will be too intense, but for some it may just be the silent revenge they need to release that anger. Do what works for you.

During or after your ceremony, pop open a bottle of champagne and celebrate! You're free! You're free to begin a new life, on your terms. Being single means you can do whatever you want. You can do all the things you wanted to do but couldn't do because of him.

This new found freedom could be as simple as lounging around in your pajamas, watching chick flicks all day. It could be the freedom to let the laundry or dishes pile up without anyone complaining. You can always find ways to celebrate freedom in everyday tasks, such as the freedom to spend your money as you see fit, to buy the groceries you love, watch the television shows you like, or the joy to walk around with no bra on. You can talk to who you want, wear what you want, and go where you want. Oh yeah, and you no longer have to shave every other day! Celebrate the freedom to do what you want. Enjoy it!

You also have the freedom to date whomever you chose. You can date younger guys, older guys, rich guys, biker guys, black guys, white guys... all kinds of men are out there to entertain you! This doesn't mean you have to go around sleeping with them. You don't have to fall in love. You don't even have to settle down with them or be anyone's girlfriend. Simply enjoy their company. (And never allow your ex to make you feel guilty about who you're dating or how often you're dating. Simply remind him that you're free to do as you please.)

Allow yourself to be free and feel the joys of the single life. It may not cure your broken heart immediately but it will distract you from the fear and pain while your heart is still healing, and that's what's most important. Then, by the time your heart has healed, you will wake up one day and realize that you're having a blast!

You may even wake up one day next to the man of your dreams. You may end up meeting the man you were truly destined to be with. You might meet your soul mate and fall madly in love, discovering a love you never dreamed possible! You may begin to look back at your ex-husband and realize he was never even worth crying about.

Purposeful Thinking

Divorce can be an exciting experience... if you allow it to be. You have to be able to push aside the fear, pain, and anger and replace it with fun, excitement, and positivity. You've got to find your positive perspective through purposeful thinking, and this takes discipline. I never said it was going to be easy. You've got to put in the work of being disciplined with your thoughts and actions on a daily basis.

Every day that passes beyond your deadline of despair you will need to purposefully push aside thoughts of loneliness and depression (or whatever negative thoughts you attribute to your divorce). You will then need to make the effort of replacing them with thoughts of being free, doing whatever you want, and discovering new things that you love.

These new thoughts could come from a variety of sources. You could replace negative thoughts with day dreaming about your dream man. They could come from silly and simple things such as being relieved of the duty of picking up your ex-husband's dirty socks and underwear off of the floor every day. Whatever it is, no matter how insignificant, find your happiness however you can.

Even if it's forced in the beginning. If it hurts so bad that you have to force the happiness, well, that's a hell of a lot better than sitting around wallowing in despair. Besides, wouldn't you rather your ex-husband see you moving on, having fun, and not caring, than for him to know you're completely heartbroken over him? Don't let him get the best of you and certainly don't allow him the pleasure of witnessing you decline without him.

When you get stuck on your ex—thoughts about what he's doing, where he's going, and who he's with—remember you're only making yourself miserable. Let it go. Walk away from the pain. That man has caused enough grief in your life. I know it seems impossible at times, but you have given him enough of your energy. Stop giving him your thoughts, focus, attention, and energy. Start giving it to yourself. The world is going to revolve around you now. Besides, the best revenge is being happy.

Celebration

Now that you've allowed yourself a dedicated chunk of time to be sad, you've hit your devastation deadline, you've had your freedom ceremony, and purposeful thinking has become less forced and more normal, allow yourself to celebrate. You've done a lot of hard work and you deserve to celebrate!

The next few years of your life are to be looked at as a celebration. You're not only celebrating your new life, you're also celebrating the fact that you're over your divorce. Here are a few suggestions of ways you can celebrate:

-Buy a new car.

-Adopt a pet or get an exotic pet.

-Do something spiritually uplifting, such as joining a church, volunteering, donating to a cause you're passionate about, or go on a mission.

-Get a tattoo or a piercing.

-Go on a road trip or take a vacation to another country.

-Get a car marker and write "Just Divorced!" on the back of your car and hang cans from strings and drive around town with your music loud and celebrate!

-Throw a divorce party!

-Fuck a hot guy for the hell of it.

-Change your style up by getting a new hair style and/or color, new makeup, or a new wardrobe.

-Enroll in college, start a new career, open a business, or do something you've always dreamed of doing.

-Throw out old furniture or decor and replace it with new stuff to get a fresh start.

-Go do something that you used to do but you stopped doing once you got married. Examples: ice skating, roller skating, going to concerts, theme parks, going to games, festivals, go surfing, skiing, biking, kayaking, etc...

-Buy a boat or a jet ski. Don't forget to take your hot guy with you and post pictures of it on Facebook.

-Start getting regular massages, pedicures, manicures, acupuncture, chiropractics or any other relaxing treatments that you may have denied yourself in the past.

The point is to do anything fun and outrageous that makes you excited about life! Celebrate your newfound freedom with joy and happiness. This will help you to shift your mindset to one of "positive change" rather than getting stuck in a mindset of "life is over." Be strong. You're a woman. There's nothing you can't handle.

Now is YOUR time. Time to discover a new life. There's much more to life out there. There's an awesome man (or two, or three, or four) out there just looking for a wonderful woman like you. If you've been married to an asshole and you're sad over the divorce, don't be sad any longer. That's like crying over the garbage man taking your trash to the dump!

Rejoice and relish in the fact that you're free to find a new man. A man that treats you well and appreciates you. A man that holds your hand, tells you you're beautiful, and wants to spend his time with you. A man that is fun to be around, makes you laugh, and loves to see you smile.

When All Else Fails

If you find it impossible to gain a positive perspective, can you at least try to change your perspective? There are people going through a lot worse. Of all the problems in the world, divorce is a tough one, but definitely not the toughest. No matter how grim your divorce may seem, no matter how much it has ruined your life, there's always someone who has it worse.

There are people dying from cancer. There are children starving to death. There are children being kidnapped, raped, molested, and murdered. Of all the terrible things going on in this world that could be happening to you, give thanks that you're in a situation that you can overcome. A situation that you know you can get out of if you truly desire to do so.

I know it's not fun to think about all the bad stuff in the

world, but sometimes you have to shift your way of thinking in order to change your mind's continual thoughts about how bad things are. Things are not that bad. Things could always be worse. Give thanks for what you do have. Make a list right now of all the wonderful things you have. On bad days, take out this list and "the things I hate about you" list and read them. Add to them whenever possible.

You may want to invite your small children to sleep with you for a few weeks while you heal. Let them know that it's not permanent, that you just need to feel their loving warmth next to you during this difficult time. They will be so happy to be sleeping with their mommy, knowing that they are making her feel a tiny bit better. Don't worry about not being able to break them of the habit when the time comes to go back to their rooms. You're the mom, and when you say it's time to go back to their room, they need to go.

Many people may disagree with this, but I don't care. As a mother, I know there's no better feeling than the love of my children. Any time I'm having a bad day or feeling down, I get my girls in bed with me and we watch movies and snuggle. Being with them takes all the pain away. These opportunities won't last forever. Children grow up way too fast. One day they won't want to snuggle with Mommy anymore. Enjoy the closeness and tenderness while it's there.

The Husband and the Whore

Is your husband or ex-husband the type that always wanted more? A man that didn't appreciate his adoring wife and beautiful home? The type of man that wasn't satisfied with all you did for him? The type that went outside of the marriage seeking sex with some slutty attention whore? This type of man is <u>never satisfied</u>. Let him go with his whore. The joke's on her...

Eventually she won't satisfy him either. I don't care if he says they're in love and getting married. It's all fun and games now, but a relationship based on cheating, lies, and deception will always crumble in the end. Simply because there was never a strong foundation to begin with... and especially with the type of man that's never satisfied.

What he doesn't realize is that looks can be deceiving. The grass is not always greener on the other side of the fence. And if it seems greener on the other side of the fence, it's because that's where all of the cows have been shitting.

Nine times out of ten, when a man leaves his wife or cheats on his wife with another woman, it always comes back to bite him in the ass. He doesn't realize it when it's happening because he's blindsided by titties. But once the new wears off and the sex gets old and the slut begins to show her true colors, the man begins to realize he made a mistake.

He gave up love for lust. That's the devil's way of breaking up the family unit. Men that fall for this type of foolish seduction always end up hurt in the end. It may not happen immediately. It may not even happen in a year or two, but eventually karma has her way of coming right back around to bite him in the ass.

This type of story usually ends with the wife being devastated while the husband and the whore are living it up and having a great time. The wife finally moving on and healing from the painful experience, while the ex-husband is beginning to realize he made a huge mistake. Then the wife officially moves on and no longer loves him.

That's when karma likes to pay her visit. That's when the whore usually leaves him for her next victim, cheats on him, gives him an STD, takes his money, and/or he finally begins to realize she's piece of shit human being. That's when the ex-husband usually comes crawling back, begging for his wife and family back. Unfortunately for him, by this time the wife has moved on and has found a new level of happiness she never knew existed.

Karma always has her way of balancing things out. This even happens when women do it to their husbands for another man. The things you do to people will eventually come back to you ten times harder. It may take years for the karma to come back around, and it always comes back around when the person who was hurt officially has healed and no longer cares!

If you're a woman that's dealing with the case of the husband and the whore... let her have him. Any man that would leave his family for a stranger is not a man. Besides, you know his true colors. You know he's not perfect. You know all of the little things he does that are downright irritating. Let her deal with that crap. You're free now. Free to pursue bigger and better things.

The Upgrade

Divorce can become a beneficial experience if you use it to your advantage. Once you've healed and you're ready to start dating again, you should consider upgrading. Men do this to us all the time. How many times do you see a man leave his wife for a younger woman, a thinner woman, or a more successful woman? It's rude of them, but they don't care. Well, we can be self-serving assholes too.

We deserve to upgrade, just like them. When you're ready to begin dating again with the intention of starting a relationship, think about what kind of man would be an upgrade for you. Don't go after the same kind of man you've always gone after. Go after someone better.

Promise yourself that you won't settle down with anyone unless he's an upgrade from your previous relationship. An upgrade could mean a variety of things. It could be a better looking man, a younger man, a more successful man, or a more intelligent man. It could be an older, wiser, and more established man or it could be a younger, more fun, and more spontaneous guy. An upgrade can mean a variety of different things, and it will be different to each woman.

Date men that are the complete opposite of your ex-husband. Think about your least favorite qualities that your ex-husband possessed, then only go after men that don't have these attributes. For example, if your ex was lazy and unmotivated, look for a man that's ambitious and successful. If your ex was a womanizer, look for a gentleman that respects women. If your ex was boring and out of shape, look for a built man that enjoys being physical and healthy.

It's time to explore life. It's time for you to get what you want. It's time for you to enjoy all of the different experiences that life has to offer. You can't enjoy or explore new and exciting experiences if you continue to date the same type of men over and over again. Now is the time to upgrade.

And, if nothing else, it will make your ex-husband mad as hell to see you with someone better than him. Happiness is the best revenge. I don't care if your ex is the one that left you and claims to no longer love you. Seeing you truly happy with another man will bother him somewhere deep down inside. Especially if that new man is the kind of man that he will never be.

Think about how it will mind fuck him to see you not only recover from his devastation, but to see you move on to bigger and better things! So, if your ex was never able to provide a comfortable lifestyle for you, make sure you move on to a man that is well off and eager to spoil you. If your ex treated you badly or cheated on you, make sure you move onto a dedicated man that is head over heels in love with you.

There are so many different men out there. The opportunities to find a great man that will introduce you to new experiences are endless. Have fun out there! Be selfish. Now is your time.

I have seen too many women be dedicated, faithful wives only to end up screwed over and hurt by their selfish husbands. It's not fair and it's time we stop selling ourselves short after divorce. Divorce is not the end. Divorce is the beginning. Having the right attitude about all of this is the key to getting through it.

Maintain the attitude that dating will be fun and exciting. Be a selfish vixen and don't feel one bit guilty about it! Tell yourself that when you're ready to love again, you will find a better man and have a great romance. A romance that will be so fun and exciting that when you look back in a few years, you will see your divorce as the greatest blessing of your life.

Even if you feel that you're too old to start again, too out of shape, or just too hurt to ever love again...remember...*that's the wrong attitude*. Never forget that you have pussy power. The world is yours! Go back and re-read book one anytime you feel full of doubt, negativity, or begin to put yourself down.

Don't ever allow the way one man treated you to discourage you from believing there are good men out there. They're out there, just waiting for a wonderful woman like you to come into their lives. Many women have moved on from divorce to fall in love with wonderful men that treat them better than they ever imagined. They've fallen deeply in love and to top it all off, the women are happier now than they ever were when they were married to their ex-husbands.

Children and Divorce

I want to take a quick moment to speak about children and divorce. I'm not a child psychologist; I'm just a child that witnessed her parents' divorce. I just wanted to take a quick moment to speak upon this deep topic from my personal perspective, because I can speak honestly about divorce from the point of view of a young child.

I have memories of my parents fighting from the time I was three years old. I was four years old when my Dad officially moved out and my Mom sold our house. They were officially divorced when I was five and she and I went to permanently live four hours away in Miami. Throughout the years I remember people who loved me worrying that the divorce may have affected me, but it didn't. I honestly have no feelings about it.

I was too young to realize what was going on. It happened at such a young age that I was accustomed to my parents being divorced. It was normal because that's all I knew. I can truly say that I appreciate the fact that my parents went through the divorce while I was very young, rather than trying to hold on for years and years, exposing me to fights and anger. I'm not saying all children will react like this; I'm just giving you some insight and perspective from a person that actually experienced and remembered their parent's divorce.

If you're a mother of young children thinking about divorce you should consider a few things. First, a separation will be much easier for your children to handle at a young age. It's much better than trying to hold on, only to end up divorced later when they're older. So, consider that if you've been continually trying to work things out, over and over again. Especially if you know in your heart that it's just not going to work.

Don't continue to try "for the sake of the children." You're not doing your kid(s) any favors by trying to hold on to your relationship simply for their sake. Children are much better off being used to their parents being separated. It's a much better alternative than being accustomed to their parents being together only to end up having to experience a traumatic separation when they're old enough to understand what's going on.

Secondly, children are much smarter than any of us think

and the older they get, the smarter and more aware they are. The longer you wait to leave, the more damage you're doing. I think older children—pre-teens, teenagers, and young adults—get hurt much, much more from divorce than younger kids. They're old enough to be accustomed to the comforts of their family unit, as well as being old enough to understand all that they're witnessing.

The best thing you can do in this situation is to sit down and talk honestly with your children. Don't wait until the last minute and catch them by surprise. Don't allow them to find out about your divorce by overhearing your discussions or arguments with your spouse or even worse by hearing it from someone other than you and your spouse.

Tell your child together with your spouse. Keep things simple and straight-forward by talking to your child on their level. You don't need to give your seven year old the same explanation that you give to your 14 year old. Don't be afraid to admit that this will be sad and upsetting for everyone.

Most importantly, don't discuss your partner's faults in front of or with the child. This is very hard to accomplish. We can all logically assume we would never trash talk the other parent in front of the kids, but that's not reality. Reality is full of blow ups, frustrations, and venting. **If you can learn to control what you say in front of your kids, no matter how much of an ass the other parent is, you will always be respected more by the kids.**

The children can see who's wrong and who's right. They will be adults one day and be able to make their own opinions about each of their parents. Don't lose your cool in a moment of anger and give them more stress at this delicate time. Hearing the wrong things about a parent can alter a child's perception. In moments of anger we tend to over exaggerate or say harsh things that we really don't mean. Don't do that to your kids. Allow them to make up their own opinions about their dad. Ask that your spouse or ex-spouse do the same.

Divorce is never easy. It's complicated, sad, and life-altering. There isn't a book or piece of advice in the world that's going to change the fact that divorce is a complex emotional event. Although you cannot escape your divorce, you can handle it in a positive way that allows you to quickly get through the pain and over to the other side of life.

Be open to what life has in store for you. Do not allow your divorce to break you. Do not allow your ex-husband to steal your right to happiness. You deserve to be happy. Allow yourself to heal, but more importantly, allow yourself to live again. Life is waiting for you...

PART TWO: MAN POWERS

Just like we have certain powers over men, there are powers that men have over us. It's a fact. We all know it. And although we may not like to admit it, we've all experienced it at one point in our lives. Some of us have been so powerless over a man that we've done foolish things that we wish we could take back or erase from our memories completely.

Unfortunately, we can't take back the past, but what we can do is recognize these powers, learn from them, and avoid them in our futures. Knowing, understanding, and recognizing the powers that men have over us is empowering in itself. When we recognize these powers we can say to ourselves, "Oh, that's just bullshit man power taking a hold of my senses. I'm not falling for that trickery!"

It's through the recognition and acknowledgment of their powers that we can gain empowerment and move on from it rather than being ignorant, being in denial, allowing it to happen, or even worse, allowing it to hold us back or dictate our lives.

In the first book I discussed two ways that men have powers over us: through our emotions and our low self-esteem. Some men have the power to MANipulate us by using these two weaknesses against us. They gain leverage into our pants, hearts, and lives. However, there are more weaknesses that we have and we all need to be aware of them.

This section of the book is made up of four chapters. Each chapter will cover a man power. Take the time to learn and recognize these powers that men can potentially have over you. Then use this knowledge as a way to get over your past, empower yourself in the present, and protect yourself in the future.

Chapter Eight

The Power of the Baby Daddy

This chapter is about deciding whether or not to leave your baby daddy alone for good. I get a lot of emails asking for help with this tough decision. Deciding to break up with the man you've created a family with isn't an easy decision. It's one that leaves many women confused and wondering what the right choice is.

On one hand you love him and want things to work for the sake of your family, and on the other hand weighs all of the crap he has put you through. What do you do? If you're one of many women that's having a hard time deciding whether or not to stay with the father of your kid(s), then this chapter is going to help guide you to the right decision. But first, this chapter is going to show you why the father of our children has power over us in the first place. Remember, acknowledging the power a man has over you is empowering in itself, so let's get to it...

The baby daddy is a man of power based solely on position. The day you got pregnant, he got a promotion and now holds an unseen power over your life. Your kid's father has power over you in three ways. You may not even know it, and he probably doesn't know it either, but whether you know it or not these three powers can form a force that's nearly impossible to break free from. These three powers are "the dream," "financial power," and "the kids." I'm going to cover each one in detail.

The Dream

The first way a baby daddy holds power over us is through "the dream." Nearly every girl grows up daydreaming about her future and what it will be like. A lot of us imagine our wedding day, our future children, and who our husband will someday be. We picture our big beautiful house, with our big beautiful family, the stylish decor we will use, the type of car we will drive, the pets we will have and so on.

We paint a pretty picture in the back of our minds of a

perfect life and a perfect FAMILY. It's not until we get older and reality sets in that we realize the perfect life isn't as easy to obtain as it seemed. Especially if you had kids with a man that turned out to be less than what you expected a man should be.

Suddenly, dreams and expectations start flying out the window. You start to expect less and less from life. Before you know it, you're wondering how you got to this point. The point of making a decision to become a single mom and leave your child's father for good. It's a terribly difficult decision to make because "the dream" holds so much power over our decisions. We don't want to let the dream die. We want to fight to the bitter end to make things work so we can have our family together.

It doesn't matter how hard you fight if the other person just isn't willing to co-operate. You can run in circles, beating your head against a wall, begging, screaming, and pleading with him to make things work for the sake of the family. However, if he isn't man enough to step up to the plate and be a responsible father, a respectful husband, and a good provider, you're wasting your energy.

You're going to have to let the good dream die and that's a reality that's hard to accept for any woman. The problem is you can't let that dream get in the way of your happiness and future. **You can't let the dream hold power over you**. This is one of the reasons why your baby daddy can have so much power over you. It's why he can be such an ass and you'll take him back time and time again. It's the good dream holding you hostage.

When you can acknowledge that holding onto the dream is a strong reason why you may be having a hard time deciding if you should leave him, then you can start to separate the dream from the reality. You can start looking at the situation with an unbiased mind by reminding yourself that the vision you held in your mind of a perfect family is just a dream; it's not reality.

It doesn't mean that it can't be a reality in the future, with another man. It's just not the reality with THIS man. That's what makes it hard though. *This man* is the father; *this man* is the one you love, but *this man* is not doing his job. Don't waste years of your life waiting for the dream to come true if you know deep down in your heart that he's never going to step up to the plate.

Financial Power

Another way that the baby daddy can have power over us and make it virtually impossible to leave him is through financial power. When we have a baby or small children at home, it can be very hard to hold a full time job. We can easily become confined to the house. Especially if we're not blessed with the help of family or friends.

When you can't work, you can easily become dependent on your child's father to provide for you and the baby, which in most cases is perfectly normal. A woman stays home with the kids, holds down the house, and the man provides for the family. However, when your baby daddy is an asshole, being financially dependent can turn into a big problem. No one wants to depend on an asshole. Assholes aren't reliable.

Nevertheless, you end up stuck. Being financially stuck is the most powerless position for a woman, especially a woman with kids. You feel like you can't escape the situation. You may feel hopeless, like there's no way out. Meanwhile, he can come and go as he pleases. He can work and make money.

By being unable to work for whatever reason while he has the freedom to make money is one of the big ways that a baby daddy can have power over you. Recognize if this is one of the powers your baby daddy may have over you. If it is, that's okay. There is a way to escape from the grips of financial power and I will go over that in a bit. For now it's just important to recognize if this type of power is crippling you.

The Kids

The final and strongest power that the baby daddy has over you isn't even his fault. Regardless it holds great power over you, so it's important to be aware of its grip. This is the power of the kids. The reason it's so strong is because there's no greater love than the love that a mother has for her child.

That undying love is what will make a mother fight to the death to protect her kids, and it will also make her do anything possible to maintain their happiness. That undeniable desire to maintain her child's happiness is what gets us into trouble, because it can be a great weakness when trying to separate from the baby daddy.

The love we have for our kids and our desire to give them the best life possible enables us to continuously try to make it work despite all of the dysfunction. That's because we assume that having Mom and Dad together is what's ultimately best for the kids. That's what will make them happy. So, we will try to make things work way beyond the point of any reason. We will defy logic. We will ignore all warnings and advice to leave the situation. All in an effort to make it work "for the kids."

This is different than the dream. This is not about *our* perfect life and visions of a happy family. This is about our *kid's lives*. This is way more important to us than any stupid dreams we had for ourselves. We can put our dreams on the back burner, but when it comes to our kids, it's not that easy. We want our babies to be happy.

We will sacrifice our own happiness to ensure their happiness. We will stay in a relationship with a bad man if we think it's for our child's best interest. We will continue the relationship way beyond the expiration date if we think it's going to provide a better future for our kids. But is it? Probably not. Especially if he's not doing his job as a man.

So, those are three powers that baby daddy can hold over you. There are probably several other factors as well, because each person's situation is unique. However, these three powers previously mentioned are the top three factors that paralyze us and keep us from moving forward. It is these three powers that usually make it difficult for us to leave our kid's father. Now that you know this, analyze your situation and ask yourself if any of these powers are holding you hostage.

Recognizing the factors that hold us back can help us to move forward with a decision and it's helpful in recognizing what holds us back. However, I know that this information is not enough to help you actually decide what to do. The next few questions are going to help you with the ultimate decision. Should you stay with your kid's father or should you leave him for good?

Should I Stay or Should I Go?

Unfortunately, when you have kids with a man, you're stuck dealing with that man for the rest of your life. People say it's for the next 18 years, but that's not true. That man is going to be around for a looooong time. One day the child you two share will probably graduate college, get married, or have children and these are all life events where you two will have to see each other again and again.

There is no escaping the baby daddy. But you can escape your relationship with him. You don't have to deal with his shit in your life, should you choose not to. Many women have moved on from the relationship with their kid's father and you can too, if that's what you want to do. But, what if you're not even sure of what you want to do? Deciding to leave a man that you have children with is complicated.

Should you stay or should you go? If that is the question, then your answers to the next seven questions will provide your answer. Make sure you answer these questions honestly. Don't make excuses for the answers you come up with, just answer the questions yes or no.

If you want to try and elicit a change from him before deciding if you should stay or leave, then I suggest you refer to the chapters "The Power of the Married Pussy" and "The Power of Food, Sex, and Loyalty." Try the techniques and suggestions in those chapters, but if all else fails, come back to this chapter.

The Seven Questions

Question One

Do you and your baby daddy fight more than you get along?

If you and your kid's dad are fighting more than you get along, this is a clear sign that things are heading in the wrong direction. If it's you against him, instead of the two of you against the world, that is a pointless relationship. Love is supposed to bring peace and harmony into your life, not bring chaos and anger. Even if you can say that it's 50/50, that is too much fighting and not enough getting along. I don't care how complicated your situation is, if fighting is a regular part of your relationship, answer yes to this question.

Question Two

Do you cry on a regular basis? If so, how often do you cry?

Crying daily, weekly, every other day, multiple times a day or even monthly is too much crying. If your man's words or actions move you to tears on a regular basis, this is a clear warning sign that you need to get out of the relationship. It's not normal to be upset and unhappy in a relationship. One of the main reasons men and women enter into relationships is to have someone there to help you through the bad times, not to be the creator of your bad times. If he makes you cry more than he makes you laugh, answer yes to this question.

Question Three

Are his "fuck ups" a regular thing?

Is he constantly fucking up and coming to you with excuse after excuse, apology after apology? Does he promise to change and never follows through on his promises? Or did he just screw up one time, beg for forgiveness, and straighten up after his wrongdoing?

If your issues revolve around his constant "mistakes," then answer yes to this question. However, if he screwed up once and you feel in your heart you can forgive him and move forward with the relationship, then you can answer no.

People make mistakes. Sometimes it takes a person making a mistake to wake up and realize that they don't ever want to make that mistake again. If you can find it in your heart to forgive, and you feel he is worthy of a second chance, then give your relationship a chance. Just remember... fool me once, shame on you, fool me twice, shame on me. DO NOT give third, fourth, fifth, or endless chances to a man just because he is the father of your child. When you give too many chances, you have no one to blame but yourself for your struggles with him.

Question Four

Is being with your kid's father holding you back in life?

If being with your kid's father is making your life harder,

rather than easier, than answer yes to this question. No one needs a partner that holds them down and makes their life more difficult. Examples of how a man can make your life harder are included, but not limited to the following circumstances.

A man that is constantly in and out of jail for whatever reasons (drugs, alcohol, violence, criminal activities, etc...) is a man that is making your life harder. A man that is constantly making stupid decisions that involve you "helping him," or a man that causes constant frustration in your life is a man that is making your life harder.

Other examples include a man that sabotages your efforts to go back to school, get a job, or work on your career. Does he refuse to grow up and move out of his parents' house so that you and he can be responsible adults? A man that won't help with bills and refuses to grow up and handle life's responsibilities is a man that is making your life harder.

Or does your man support you, encourage you, and want you to succeed in life? Does he uplift you and bring out the best in you? Does he co-operate in your efforts to maintain a household for your family? Does he pay his fair share of bills, and/or do his fair share of the child care and cleaning?

Have you ever heard of the saying, "I can do bad all by myself?" If you're with a man that is making your life more difficult by being a part of it, that is a sure sign that you need to move on. Life will be easier on your own.

If this feels like your situation then ask yourself a few more questions and answer them honestly: How long can you continue to pick up the slack for him before you break down? How long will you wait for him to change before it's too long? Set an exact time frame of how much of your life you're willing to sacrifice for him.

If you find that you can't walk away from him now, then at least if you have answered those questions, you have set an exact time frame for how long you're willing to wait for him to change. Make a promise to yourself that if he has not changed by these dates, then you will leave, no matter what.

Question Five

Does he want to be with his friends more than he wants to be with his family?

This is a big red flag of immaturity. A man will want to be at home with his wife and kids as much as possible. Sure, men hang out with their friends, but if his priorities are spending time with his friends over you and the baby, then you're being shafted. No woman should have to sit around waiting for her man to spend quality time with her and their kid(s).

You should not be sitting home alone on a regular basis, stuck in the house, while he is out enjoying freedom and partying. That's not fair to you; it's not fair to your child, and it's a big sign pointing to where his priorities are in life. If you're willing to sit at home waiting for him to show you some love and attention and you don't mind that you and your kid are second in his life, then by all means, stay with him. However, I know and you know that no woman wants to be second place to a man's friends.

Question Six

Is he an alcoholic or a drug addict?

If the answer to this question is yes, then you need to be VERY careful about how much time you invest into this man before giving up. Some men can stop, get clean, and remain sober and productive. However, some men cannot. You don't want to waste 20 years of your life hoping and waiting for him to sober up, only to find out that he cannot let it go.

You need to be aware of the disease of addiction and just

how powerful it can be, because it can rob you of many years of your life. Years wasted trying to support him and help him, only to end up later in life with a full blown crack head, drunk, meth junkie, or pill poppin' animal for a husband. Pay attention to his habit and take notice if he can't control it. You don't want to get you and your children's lives caught up in the middle of that storm.

You can start out by supporting him and being there for him in an attempt to help him escape the grips of addiction, but you need to set a time limit on how long you're willing to wait for him to get well. Don't tell him this time limit. Watch and wait, and if he does not clean up in a reasonable amount of time, then you need to move on with your life, without him, because he will drag you down... if you let him.

Question Seven

Is there abuse in the relationship?

Is there any form of abuse occurring in your relationship? Abuse refers to more than just physical abuse. Abuse comes in many different forms, such as verbal, sexual, mental, financial, or a combination of these. Some of you may be thinking, "No shit, being abused in any way is wrong and is an automatic sign that you need to leave a relationship." But, it's not such an easy decision to make for the woman being abused.

It can be hard for a woman to answer yes to this question, either because she doesn't want to admit that there is abuse (because then she would have to leave and she doesn't want to) or because she doesn't even recognize her man's behavior as abuse. I'm going to cover the different forms of abuse so that your answer to this question can be clear and definite.

A woman does not end up in an abusive relationship by accident. Abusers look for women that will be easy to control. They look for certain characteristics about a woman's personality, such as having very low self-esteem, being naïve, and/or being a very giving, nurturing woman. Having these characteristics can sometimes be an invitation for a man that abuses women. Not every woman will tolerate abuse, so an abuser must seek out the woman who is willing to accept it.

Abuse is More Than a Slap in the Face

Abuse comes in many forms. Some forms of abuse may be hard to recognize as abuse. Physical abuse is much easier to recognize than emotional or financial abuse. You may not even think you're being abused. There's no bruises. You haven't been hit. When a man hits you, it's a clear sign that he is abusing you.

However, some other forms of abuse—such as mental, emotional, financial, or sexual abuse—are not as easy to recognize. You may just think your man has an anger problem, control issues, or he's just a very jealous guy. I'm going to briefly cover each of these other, less talked about forms of abuse so that you can evaluate if you're being abused in any way.

Financial Abuse

I talked a little bit about this earlier, and I said I would go into more detail. Before I begin, I just want to mention that a baby daddy having financial power over you is not the same as abusing you financially. There is a fine line between depending on a man financially because you can't work and a man that uses that dependency against you.

If you're with a man that knows you depend on him for food, shelter, clothing, transportation and the needs of the children and *he uses that against you,* or *uses it as an excuse to be cruel or mean to you,* or *he controls your money and how you spend it,* that's financial abuse. Some people have learned how to use money as leverage. They know you don't have a way of taking care of yourself and you depend on them, so they feel they can treat you any kind of way they want, knowing you have to tolerate it.

Financial abuse can also happen when a man relies on you for all financial needs and controls all of your spending. He could be taking your check every week and dictating where and how it's spent. He could be racking you up with debt, forcing you to borrow money, take loans, or even convincing you to pawn all of your stuff. All of this leaves the woman drained, without a pot to piss in, forcing her to be even more dependent on the relationship.

This can happen even more so to a woman who has children with someone. Since we're the caretakers of the children, we have to stay home and can't work. This disables us and makes us dependent on our partner to take care of us. There's absolutely nothing wrong with that if you have a loving, supportive partner and you're both happy. But, if your partner uses this as an excuse to demean and demoralize you, or if he uses it as a way to make you do things you don't want to do, or to keep you imprisoned and enslaved to him, that's abuse.

Sexual Abuse

Everyone has the right to decide what they do or don't want to do sexually. Not all sexual assaults are violent "attacks." Most victims of sexual assault know the assailant. Sexual abuse can occur between two people who have been sexual with each other before, including people who are *married or dating*.

Just because you're in a relationship with someone does not give them the right to force you to have sex, although they may think that it gives them the right to force sex upon you. To many of us this may seem obvious, but I guarantee that there is someone out there reading this book that is being sexually abused by her man. She may suspect that what he is doing is wrong, but may doubt herself because they are in a relationship and she loves him.

You could be sexually abused and not even realize it because you assume sexual abuse simply involves being raped. There is far more to it than that. Sexual abuse is any time someone (whether he is your boyfriend, husband, or stranger) convinces you, coerces you, intimidates you or forces you to do something sexual that you don't want to do.
It goes even further than that. Sexual abuse can also occur when someone inhibits your ability to control your sexual activity, such as unwanted kissing or touching, unwanted rough sex or violent sexual activity, unwanted sex or sexual activities taking place while you're drunk or sleeping, and even pressuring you to have sex with other people, such as undesired threesomes.

All of these scenarios can go beyond just sex, and can include oral sex, anal sex, rape, molestation, harassment, and they can even go as far as restricting your access to birth control or even worse, denying your requests to use condoms or protect yourself from STD's. This all is considered sexual abuse.

Verbal, Mental, and Emotional Abuse

Verbal, mental, and emotional abuse are much harder forms of abuse to recognize because they are more psychological than physical and tangible. I have put these forms of abuse all into the same category because they are all meant to play mind games. They're all an attempt to make you feel like worthless shit and directly attack your self-esteem, self-worth, and sense of wellbeing.

I discussed one form of mental abuse in the first book when I covered the topic of the insecure man. The insecure man uses insults and puts his woman down in an attempt to make her think that no man will want her but him. In reality, it's his own low self-esteem that creates a fear of losing her, and it's that fear that perpetuates this nonsense.

If he was confident and knew he was a great guy, he would not fear losing her and therefore would lift her up and compliment her. Besides, if he really felt all of those negative things were true, why would he be with her? It's all just psychological mind games that prey on our low self-esteem. The insecure man is using verbal, mental, and emotional abuse to keep his woman by his side.

Verbal abuse is when someone says derogatory things to you that are mean and hateful. A man that calls you stupid, ugly, fat, or any other verbal insult with the intention to hurt your feelings is verbally abusing you. I'm not talking about getting in a fight and slinging curse words at one another. I'm referring to the man that purposely and intentionally spews out mean and degrading words at his woman.

Verbal abuse can also cause emotional abuse because the derogatory insults are made in an attempt to hurt your feelings. But emotional abuse can also occur with no words. For instance, a man that ignores you on purpose and makes you feel like you're not important. A man that makes you feel as if he can't stand to be around you. A man that withholds affections, such as kisses and hugs. Again, this is all to cause you to feel like you don't matter or to make you feel like you're a terrible person unworthy of love.

Mental abuse is a form of abuse that plays with your mind. It includes examples such as a man that attempts to force you to give up friends, keep you away from your family, or convince you to believe that there's no one else but him that truly loves and cares about you. It could also go the opposite way by making you feel that you're not good enough for anyone and deserve the treatment you're getting.

Some of these forms of abuse may be obvious to some of you, however, there are a lot of women dealing with this type of treatment on a regular basis. A lot of them don't even realize that they are being abused. This type of treatment may seem normal to them either because 1) it's all they've ever known; they come from abusive families and so it's normal behavior to them, or 2) because their self-esteem is so low that they become crippled by the abuse.

If you're staying with a man that abuses you, you need to ask yourself these very serious questions: Why do you feel it's okay to be with a man that abuses you? Were you raised in an abusive environment, so it's normal behavior to you, and perhaps that's why you're accepting of it? Are you using "I love him" as an excuse to allow him to continue on his path of abuse? Sorry, but I've said it before and I will say it again: love is just not enough of an excuse to stay with a man that treats you badly.

What to Do If You Have Nowhere to Turn

If you recognize your situation in any of these examples of abuse, or you're simply stuck, there are things you can do. You don't have to feel alone, isolated, and out of options. One thing you can do is plan to leave him without his knowledge. He doesn't have to know that you're planning to leave him for good until after you've already left.

Begin making plans and set a time frame. It could be as far away as a year. In that time frame you begin to prepare by saving money, even if you can only save a few dollars here and there. Go to school if you can, so that when you're ready to leave, you have the education you need to support yourself. Begin informing your closest and most trusted family and friends of your plans to leave for good and ask them for ideas and suggestions.

Gather child support documents, information about filing for divorce, obtaining alimony, food stamps, cash assistance or any other form of support that will help you in your transition. Then sit down and make a plan that is reasonable and executable. Get all your ducks in a row and then one day, when he least expects it, you leave and you leave for good. There is no turning back.

If the abuse is really bad and/or you have nowhere to go, no money, and no one to help you, you can always go to a women's shelter. They have women's shelters all over the country. These shelters are specifically designed for women who need a safe place to run to, so that they can start their lives over independently. You don't have to be physically abused to seek help from a woman's shelter. As I mentioned earlier, abuse comes in many forms, and these shelters will help women suffering from any form of abuse.

This website can direct you to a shelter in your area. http://www.womenshelters.org. You can also dial 211 from any phone to get connected to local social services. Tell them briefly of the problem you're facing and ask them if they can direct you to the proper services. In addition to shelters and other social services, the Catholic Church is known to help assist women and children as well. There are people out there to help you escape a bad situation, should you choose to leave. **You never have to feel stuck.**

Services like these were created for women and children because of the dependency that I spoke about earlier. If a woman is dependent upon someone that abuses her, how would she ever be able to escape the situation? It's nearly impossible, especially if she doesn't have friends and family to help her. Communities have recognized this unique issue that women face and have come together to form support systems to help transition women and children out of abusive or unwanted situations. Take advantage of the help that is available for you, should you need to escape an abusive man.

Pros and Cons

So, you answered all of the questions and you're still not sure if you should stay or you should leave your kid(s) father? The last tool you have to help you decide is the pros and cons list. The pros and cons list has helped people make some of the toughest life decisions. You can use it for just about any conflicted decision in life.

Take a piece of paper or go to your journal and draw a line down the center. On one side write "Pros" and on the other column write "Cons." Under the pros list, you're going to write down all of the good things about this man and your relationship. Write down anything you can think of, from the big things to the little things. In the cons list, write down all of the bad things about this man and your relationship.

Get it all out on paper. Even if you think it's insignificant. You can even write down situations that happened, whether good or bad. Give credit where credit is due, but don't be in denial about the bad stuff. Write it all down until you can't think of anything else left to write down. Fill up multiple pages if you need to. Once you feel that you've gotten it all out on paper, then you can clearly see if this relationship has more bad than good, or more good than bad.

If the cons list is longer than the pros, then your answer is obvious. If the pros out way the cons, then perhaps your relationship has hope. Now that you have answered all of the questions and you have listed all of the pros and the cons of your relationship, you should have a clear picture of what the right choice is. But what if the right choice is a move that you just can't bring yourself to make?

Your Answer

If you know in your heart it's time to move on, but you're having a hard time with your answer, then take this moment to analyze your situation. Think about all of the hardships this man has put you and your kid(s) through. Then take a moment to imagine life without him. Either scenario is going to have its ups and downs. Then think about it this way... if you decide to stay with him, then you will be spending more years of your life waiting and hoping that he's going to change. *What if he never changes?*

What if you wait and an entire decade goes by and he's still the same? What if you wait for so long that your children have grown up witnessing him and his bad behavior? What if they become so accustomed to it that your daughters grow up and have children with a man just like him? What if your sons learn his behavior and grow up to treat their kid's mother the same way?

Of course that's not what any woman hopes for her children. However, the chances of that happening are very high the longer you stay with someone. You teach your children how to interact with the opposite sex by how you interact with the opposite sex. If they see their mother puts up with a lot of crap from Dad, they're going to grow up thinking that is normal behavior.

However, if they see Mom putting her foot down and not tolerating crap from a man by leaving a bad man and starting a new life, then they're going to grow up to be people that don't tolerate bad treatment as well. They will also gain a lot of respect for you for doing what was necessary, regardless of how hard the decision was.

No one is saying it's going to be easy. However, you will get through it and you will figure out a way to make it on your own. There are plenty of women who've had children with someone, had to break up, and have made it work.

Just because you have kids with someone is not an excuse to stay and put up with their bullshit. If your baby's father is lying, cheating, or mistreating you in any way, don't use the kids as an excuse to put up with bad behavior. That's giving him way too much power over your life.

If you know in your heart that things are never going to change, then be woman enough to admit that to yourself. Be strong enough to do something about it. Sure, it will be hard without him. Being a single mother is not easy. In fact, I believe it's one of the hardest jobs out there. But you know what's harder than being a single mom? Being with a man that treats you badly, crying over a man on a regular basis, and feeling all alone even though you're supposed to be in a relationship.

Chapter Nine

The Power of Mr. Good Dick

Every woman appreciates a man that knows how to make her toes curl. But, watch out! The power of Mr. Good Dick can make the smartest woman in the world act like a damn fool. You better beware, beware, beware... of a man that can lay the pipe. Mr. Good Dick can override your pussy powers in a heartbeat, if you let him. You must use caution and self-control at all times.

Even worse than Mr. Good Dick is the Mr. Good Dick that knows how to play games with the dick. These are the worst ones. These are the ones that have left women confused, bamboozled, and heartbroken.

She didn't even see it coming, but before she knows it, she's doing things completely out of character. She's driving around town following the dick. She's stalking the dick on Twitter. She's fighting a bitch over the dick. She's lost control of her emotions and is stuck on a path of foolishness, all for that dick.

Mr. Good Dick has power, and lots of it, but remember *he only has the power that you allow him to have.* If you use good judgment and maintain self-control, you can override his penis power. Don't allow yourself to get drunk off the dick. Enjoy it and have fun, but like any indulgence in life, you need to know when to say no and walk away. Too much of anything is a bad thing, and the same goes for good sex. Just because something is good, doesn't mean it's good for you.

You should never allow anyone or anything to cloud your thinking, turn you into a fool, or sabotage your sanity. Control those emotions! Good sex can bring on a whirlwind of emotions and these uncontrolled, sexually driven emotions can easily override your common sense. This is how the smartest and most responsible women end up in stupid situations.

These bad situations can end with getting pregnant, becoming severely heartbroken, fighting with another woman over a man, and in the worst case, contracting a sexually transmitted disease. That's how easily Mr. Good Dick can come into your life and fuck things up.

Be careful not to fall in love with Mr. Good Dick. You may be setting yourself up for future heartache. How do you think he got so good? Practice makes perfect. He got good from slinging that dick all over town!

Using Mr. Good Dick

Poor Mr. Good Dick, I'm giving him a bad image. But, I will admit, he's not always a bad thing. In some cases, his powers can be used for good. You know when Mr. Good Dick can be a positive force in your life? When you've just been dumped or you're recently divorced and you're having a really hard time getting over your ex. Or perhaps, if you've been single for a while and need to put some spunk back into your life.

Mr. Good Dick can be really helpful for getting over a rough patch in life. He can distract your mind from the pain. He can entertain you. He can even be used to make your ex super jealous. Cougars can seek young dicks for a thrilling evening. Cougar cubs can seek older men for some experience and spoiling.

Break away from what you're used to. Try something different. You're not going to marry Mr. Good Dick. You just want to have fun with him. Mr. Good Dick is an escape from reality, a nice break from the norm. You just have to be careful not to let it go and get you all stupid. Don't allow your emotions to consume you.

The Curious Case of Mr. Good Dick

The problem with good dick, besides being strong enough to withstand its powers, is knowing when to walk away. Walking away from a passionate love affair is not easy. It seems almost impossible. It's like you're high off love and it clouds your judgment. It harms your ability to think clearly about the situation. It disables your strength. Add a strong history or kids into the mix and it really gets tough to make a wise decision. What to do? What to do? When do you say enough is enough and leave Mr. Good Dick alone?

When you get down to the root of this problem, you're really just torn between two things. You want the companionship of a loyal man who wants to spend his time with you, a man that will commit and love you unconditionally. However, you want it from *this* man. The man that knows how to lay the pipe, get your heart pounding and your panties wet but who may not be willing to give you that committed relationship or at least not the way you want it.

There's only one way to solve this conundrum. You're going to have to decide what you really want in life. Do you want great sex or do you want great love? The chances of you finding both, without compromising your sanity, are slim. Sure, you can find both, but it may not be that passionate gorilla pounding sex. Sorry, but it's reality.

It's only reality because our minds like to play tricks on us. The fact of the matter is that our desire to want what we can't have is the driving force that misleads us into these traps. A subconscious and foolish trap that dulls our senses and leads us to believe we're unable to have both.

We are silly. When a man *wants* to be with us and *wants* to love us, it makes the sex less thrilling and stimulating. It's really not so much about one guy being bad in bed and the other guy being so awesome as much as it's the high we get from achieving something that was a bit of a challenge.

We all want what we can't have. The fact that Mr. Good Dick doesn't want to give you the commitment you want makes him more thrilling. It's an emotional roller coaster filled with ups and down. When things are bad, you're on a low but every time you get the dick, or get your way with him, you're on a high and it feels awesome. It's that thrill ride of emotions that makes the sex so much better.

It's a false sense of excitement and unfortunately it's at the expense of sacrificing what you really want in a man. Don't let the high of chasing Mr. Good Dick mislead you into thinking his dick is what's got you hooked. It could simply be the up and down highs of the mind games that have got you psychologically addicted to his penis. It's not the actual penis! It's the games played by the owner of the penis! Just like "The Power of the Pussy" isn't really about the pussy; it's about the thrill of hunting, chasing, and capturing the pussy that makes the man sprung.

So, if you're currently dealing with a curious case of Mr. Good Dick, and you're not sure of what to do, let me ask you a few things. Be honest with yourself when answering the following questions and know that there are no right or wrong answers.

#1) Are you willing to wait and see if he's going to commit or change?

If you can honestly say yes to this question, then wait it out and see if you can eventually get what you want out of the relationship. However, you need to put a deadline on how long you're willing to wait. (See next question)

Before walking away, you can always take the chance of using "Just Say It" (telling him bluntly yet sweetly what it is that you want). Put it all out on the line and hope he gives you what you want. Maybe he can't fully commit, but he would be willing to at least give you some of what you want. See how far he is willing to go or how much he will give and then decide from there if you're willing to take his offer. And if he can't give anything, well, then at least you know where he stands.

Be warned, using "just say it" also means taking a big gamble on the heartache that could come if he refuses or is unwilling to give you what you want. Let alone the embarrassment of putting yourself out there and finding out that he doesn't feel the same. For some it will be worth it and for others it will be best to walk away.

#2) If so, how long are you willing to wait?

Set a date. Put a deadline on it. I don't care if it's weeks or months. The amount of time you're willing to invest is up to you. Don't subject yourself to any more of the dick drama beyond that date. Stick to it. Promise yourself you will walk away on this day if things have not changed. Most importantly, don't go back on your word when the day comes.

#3) Are you willing to sacrifice some of the qualities you want in a relationship or that on your dream man list for great sex?

If yes, then be with him, but you will have no one but yourself to blame if things turn out bad or don't go the way you want them. You can't get mad at him. You made the sacrifice and you will have to live with your decision. If this is your choice, that's fine. Just remember that you were the one that chose to settle for less in exchange for sex.

#4) Is his penis really *that* special?

Come on, be honest. Is it really that big of a deal? There isn't a man on this planet that's so incredibly awesome in bed that it's worth stressing over. There's plenty of other fish in the sea that know how to fuck just as good or even better than he can. Besides, anything a man can do for you, you can do for yourself (and probably a lot better).

And if it really is *that* special, but he's the type that finds it difficult to commit or stay faithful, then you're in for a roller coaster ride of drama and frustration. Are you willing to live in constant turmoil or fight with other girls for your Mr. Good Dick?

#5) **Have you been tricked by your inexperience?**

You may think you're fucking the greatest lover on the planet, but if he's your first or second lover, what the hell do you know? How do you know there isn't a better lover out there for you? One who may be more passionate, romantic, giving, or wild in bed?

#6) **Can you enjoy the sex for a few more weeks and then move on?**

If yes, then allow yourself to have fun for a bit longer. Use him for sex, but be prepared with a deadline of when you will walk away from the passionate love affair. Set a date on the calendar. This is your dick deadline. After that date, walk away, no matter what the circumstances are at that time.

If no, then stop right now and refer back to book number one for help in moving past this love affair. Or, accept that you've got a problem on your hands and by sticking around you're probably going to end up sacrificing your own happiness,wants, and needs to be with this man. The longer you stay involved with him the harder it's going to be to move on. So, be careful and don't allow yourself to get stuck in a sinking sand pit of lust.

Dick Decisions:
Why Does This Have to be So Hard?

Deciding when and whether or not to walk away from your love affair with Mr. Good Dick isn't easy. It's all up to what you can take emotionally. We know that we're emotional beings and our actions are motivated by our feelings. If you know in your heart that you're not going to be emotionally strong enough to walk away, then don't continue to dig yourself deeper and deeper into the emotional hole by investing more time and energy (and good sex) into the relationship.

It can be hard to walk away from the men that do give us those good feelings because they're hard to find. Let's be honest, not every man you date is going to knock your socks off. But, are those good feelings equal to the bad feelings of loneliness or sadness? That's what you have to keep in mind at all times. You have to outweigh the good for the bad.

Perhaps another man won't give you that level of excitement, but he also won't give you bad feelings. What's more important to you? You have to figure that one out, and neither answer is wrong. Some people prefer passion and lust over love and trust. Of course, in a perfect world, we want it all. Well, contrary to popular belief... you can have it all! You just have to go about it the right way. The wise way.

Finding the full package is attainable. You can find him. He's out there. You just have to be smart, patient, and diligent in your search. Finding your perfect man requires two very important skills from you. The first skill requires that you do not settle down easily. The second skill requires that you do not get tied up in a man that's not the full package.

If you get wrapped up and focused on the wrong man for the wrong reasons then you're distracted. When you're distracted you will miss out on Mr. Perfect because you're consuming all of your time and energy on Mr. Good Dick or some other unworthy man. So, have fun with Mr. Good Dick, but don't get consumed by his penis powers to the point of allowing him to distract you from your ultimate goal of finding the full package in Mr. Perfect.

Don't Slip

ALWAYS ALWAYS ALWAYS use protection and take precautions. We all know this. We've heard it 1,000 times. However, you know and I know that in the heat of the moment, sometimes passion overrides logic. Intense passion can cause us to stop thinking clearly and lead us to make very stupid decisions. Then we have to walk around paranoid until we get to the doctor to get tested. Then we torture ourselves waiting for the results. Then, if we're lucky, we get a pass and find out we're clean.

But for some that are not so lucky, they get the most devastating news of their life. You don't want to go there. Not for some dick. It's just not worth it. Our bodies are precious, not a dumping ground for man pleasure. Act accordingly.

Do not have unprotected sex, or unprotected oral sex, whether it's him giving it to you or you giving it to him. The next time you're in the heat of the moment passion and you find yourself about to make a foolish decision to have unprotected sex, I want you to envision a picture in your head. I want you to think of the chlamydia, herpes, or syphilis hiding beneath the surface of his penis, just waiting for some gullible girl to come along and give it a new home.

You can't see these diseases, and the reality is that one in four people have an STD. That's pretty fucking scary! So, you're better off assuming that everyone has one than making the assumption that this one time you'll be okay. Don't let lust, passion, or your hormones get the best of you and allow you to make a decision that could end up changing your life forever. Mr. Good Dick is never THAT good!

Make a promise to yourself that from now on you will only have unprotected sex with a man after you've both decided to be monogamous, gone to the clinic together, and been tested. If you're waiting sixty days to have sex with a man, you will have developed the relationship enough to where this shouldn't even be an issue. It's a matter of respecting your body, and if he respects you, he will not have an issue with getting tested.

This can also be a way to utilize the Prince Charming Test. If a man cares about you, he will want to make you feel comfortable. He will want to appease you, and therefore he won't mind doing this favor for you.

Make sure you see the test results with your own eyes. In addition, don't be pressured or tricked into believing that he just got tested and he's clean, or fall for the "you don't trust me?" guilt. Don't believe that you or your partner are not at risk because you're older, you're inexperienced, you don't sleep around, or for any other reasons. Sexually transmitted diseases don't discriminate.

It's also important that you both clearly ask to be tested for all sexually transmitted diseases, including chlamydia and herpes. All states are different, but I know that in some states you have to specifically ask for everything, or else they will just do a basic test that only covers HIV, syphilis, and gonorrhea. To find free or discounted testing centers or for more information about STD testing visit http://hivtest.cdc.gov or http://www.itsyoursexlife.com.

Chapter Ten

The Power of Rejection

Do you know one of the main reasons why the baby daddy, Mr. Good Dick, and men in general have the potential to have so much power over us? The power of rejection. Rejection is a powerful force because it can completely disable, retard, and defunct our power to control our emotions. It's paralyzing.

Both women and men alike have the potential to inflict the power of rejection upon the opposite sex. However, for the sake of this book, I'm going to cover why rejection is so damn powerful, how rejection from men affects us, and what we can do to overcome its emotional grips.

Why is Rejection so Powerful?

Anytime a person is rejected—for whatever reason, whether it's concerning family matters, peers at school, friends, business, or love—that rejection can wreak havoc on the emotions. It's painful. It's almost like an internal bruise. Ask anyone suffering from rejection and they will tell you the emotional pain hurts more than if they would have suffered a physical injury. Anyone in pain is going to seek immediate relief. **It's that desire for immediate relief that gives rejection its power.**

It's a force that's very insignificant to the person doing the rejecting, but has the potential to devastate the person being rejected. Sometimes rejection is so strong that it can make us devastated over losing a guy we didn't even like that much in the first place! If you're heartbroken over a guy that rejected you, ask yourself if it's really the loss of the guy that's hurting you, or is it the pain of being rejected?

If you realize that you're hurting over a guy you didn't like that much to begin with, then for sure rejection is the real culprit. If you can recall that you didn't even care that much about this dude until he rejected you, then you need to check yourself. Remind yourself that you weren't even that interested until he pulled the plug. Had you pulled the plug, you may not have thought twice about it. You're allowing a man to have power over you simply because he rejected you.

How Does Rejection Affect Us?

Rejection affects us in many ways, but when it comes to love and men, a lot of us are making decisions solely based on the intention of feeling better. Then we end up doing things we regret just to get immediate relief from rejection. However, some of us are reacting to a much deeper and more detrimental level of rejection and its cousin, abandonment.

Abandonment and rejection from the men in our lives can cause us to do stupid things. Whether that rejection or abandonment is deep seated emotional baggage from a father or recent rejection from a man we love(d), in either case it causes internal damage and leads us to act and react based on pain and fear.

The pain from the rejection and the fear of the pain occurring again affect us on levels we may not even be aware of. For some of us it could lead to accepting crap from a man over and over again. For some it may lead to being promiscuous. For others the complete opposite happens. We end up shutting people out, shutting people down, and avoiding love at all costs. Of course rejection isn't the only reason for people to behave these ways, but it is a major factor.

However, when it comes to love and relationships, rejection is at its fiercest and has the ability to quickly destroy a woman's power. That's why the power of rejection is on the list of powers that men have over us. We must be aware of it, because knowing it's out there is half the battle.

How to Overcome Rejection

So, now that we're aware of the havoc that rejection can have on us, let's get to the most important part: getting over it.

Recognition: It's important to always be on the lookout for the power of rejection. It can sneak up on you at any moment. When it hits, it can override a woman's pussy power in a heartbeat. Rejection has the power to motivate us to do stupid things we never imagined ourselves doing. It can cause the strongest woman to break down her walls of strength. It has the power to leave us feeling weak, inferior, and defenseless. Rejection is a mother fucker.

Recognize when rejection is having power over you. The awareness is where the empowerment lies. When you can recognize it, you can do something about it. Such as rejecting the rejection, controlling your emotions, and deciding not to allow it to have power over you.

Don't Take It Personally: It's not really the person, the fight, the break up, or whatever element is surrounding the rejection that's hurting so deeply. It's the rejection itself. That's what's causing so much emotional destruction. But why is rejection such an intense emotion? Why is it so devastating?

The first obvious reason why is because rejection is taken *very personally.* We tell ourselves, "There's got to be something wrong with me. Why else would he not want to be with me anymore?" Then comes a slew of internal insults. "I'm not good enough. I'm not sexy enough. I'm not pretty enough. I AM NOT ENOUGH." It creates a void. It can leave one feeling empty. It completely crushes our confidence and is a major blow to the ego.

This blow to your confidence can make it impossible to let go of a man that has rejected you. Your ego is searching for comfort and re-assurance. This search for comfort is the cause for a lot of problems, because it makes walking away very hard. We don't want to let it go until we get the re-assurance, the comfort, or the repair to the ego that we need. The only way to get that comfort is for the man to change his mind and come back. When this doesn't happen, it can take weeks or even months to recover from the internal emotional wounds of rejection.

There's one sure way to get over the pain of rejection, and that's to not take it personally. Which can be hard to do because we automatically internalize it. We *allow* the situation to make us feel unworthy and unlovable. Then we fall into the terrible trap of believing something is wrong with us. All of this negative self-talk can lead to depression and low self-esteem. Be careful with rejection. Don't allow it to lead you down a path of self-loathing. Once you're walking down that path, it can be hard to get off.

Suddenly, you're walking around all gloomy and down. You're not being yourself. You may even be hiding in bed, shunning the world and everyone in it. This can lead to missed opportunities. Opportunities to meet new men who will take your mind off of Mr. Rejection. If you can recognize this emotion for what it is, and *decide* to not take it personally, and *decide* not to internalize it, you can get over rejection much faster.

Think about this: there may have been a time in your life when you rejected someone. It probably hurt him terribly, but you may not have thought much about it. What seems like the end of the world to one person can seem like no big deal to the one who is doing the rejecting.

Try your hardest not to take rejection personally. Half of the time when a man rejects you, it's not really about you personally, and if it is, then fuck him. Who cares? He doesn't define your self-worth. You do. Don't allow him to have that power.

Rejection is redirection: A lot of the time, rejection is for your own good. You were not meant to be with that person. God has put you on a different path to meet the man you're destined to be with.

How many times have we heard the story of a woman or man that was left devastated by the one they loved only to heal from the pain, move on, and find their soul mate? They always end up finding someone better. Rejection is for one's own good, but too often we're left so devastated over it that we can't even begin to imagine something positive is to come from it.

Reject the rejection: You can escape the grips of rejection by beating it at its own game. Reject it! Do not let the pain and fear of rejection get the best of you. Do not to take it personally. Do not internalize it. Do not dwell on it. Take it for what it is: a chance to move on to bigger and better things. A push in the right direction. A direction that's leading you to your destiny. Remember, rejection is only an emotion. An emotion that has a lot of unnecessary strength and can overpower you... *if you let it*.

Chapter Eleven

The Power of the Patriarchy

"'I've never been able to find out precisely what feminism is. I only know that people call me a feminist whenever I express sentiments that differentiate me from a doormat or a prostitute." ~Rebecca West (Author)

This is the last chapter of the book because patriarchy is by far the most powerful force used against women. Patriarchy is defined as a male dominated society, one in which men are mainly in control and hold the more powerful positions. This is a very deep, intricate, and controversial discussion. One that can't be covered in a few paragraphs, a chapter, or even an entire book. So, I'm just going to write about my thoughts and opinions on the subject. I'm going to cover a lot in this chapter. It's going to be controversial. It's politically incorrect, and things are going to get ugly.

It's my opinion that right now is an important time in history. There's no better time for us to be aware of the power of the patriarchy. I'm going to explain how and why in a moment. I'm also going to explain how and why the power of the patriarchy causes women a great amount of unnecessary grief. How it cripples our power, confuses us, conditions us, controls us, takes advantage of us, and how all of this affects society as a whole. More importantly, what we can do to stop it.

Although we've come a long way over the past few decades because of the women's revolution, patriarchy still has its ways of dominating women... and the world. (It's not just women that suffer from the grips of control that the patriarchy holds. Men suffer as well, and I will explain why later.) Unfortunately, despite the revolution, the patriarchy is still alive and well.

The patriarchy may never die, but it sure would be a welcome change to see what the world would be like if women were the leaders. Honestly, it's going to take a woman's touch to rescue this planet from the on-going destruction. Women are natural born nurturers, so perhaps what the world needs now is some tender love and care.

What would happen if women ran the world? Would there finally be world peace? Would the environment get the love, attention, and care that it so desperately needs and deserves? Would the fierce gap in incomes worldwide that causes one man to be a billionaire while another man starves begin to close? Or would life go on as it is today?

Some would jokingly say that bombs would drop at the first signs of PMS. Even if that were the case, we would still be in better hands. At least we would think of all the human lives at risk and the toll it would take on the environment before pushing the button! Our compassion and instincts to nurture would override any PMS impulses, believe me. Besides, the patriarchy has had its fair share of time to figure this stuff out and apparently it's been getting nowhere fast.

Ladies, as I mentioned earlier, we're living in a very important time. We're the generation that's experiencing the beginning fazes of a transition out of patriarchy and into a more balanced society, perhaps even into a matriarchy. For the first time in history, more women than men are graduating from college. More women than ever are taking powerful roles in high-paying positions within the business world. Thanks to the recession, the amount of women that are the bread winners of their families is on the rise. It appears that women are taking the lead.

There are powerful women all over the world making history for becoming their country's first female president. I wouldn't doubt if America will soon see its first female president if Hillary Clinton decides to run in the next election. (And might I add that if she wins, I hope she gets some head in the oval office from an intern that looks like Channing Tatum. Two can play at that game, gentlemen.)

We've come a long way. In less than 100 years, we've gone from not being allowed to vote all the way to being voted into powerful positions. Despite how far we've come, we still have a bit further to go. We need to be able to recognize the faulty aspects of today's patriarchy and work together to improve things for all human beings.

These next few sections are going to point out some examples of the issues that exist in today's patriarchy. See if you recognize any of your life's experiences in the following pages. It's important to acknowledge the issues created by this male dominated society, because when we're aware of it, we can work together to change it. One of the first places I want to start is regarding the intentional suppression of our God given powers.

Dude, Where's My Pussy Power?

There are people out there that don't want women to realize that they have power... and lots of it. Why else did the women of the past have to fight so hard for equality? Why else do women around the world still face resistance when fighting for equal rights? If we aren't a threat, then what's the big deal? Another reason I came to this conclusion was regarding all of the backlash I received from the first book.

I thought I was just releasing an empowering dating advice book. Little did I know I was about to be attacked. Insults and labels were thrown around—such as feminist, misogynist, sexist, man-hater, whore, slut, and so forth. Well, which one is it? Am I a feminist or a misogynist? Am I a man-hater or a slut? I certainly can't be all of those things at once. And is it really such a crime to encourage women to wait a bit longer to have sex or to fall in love with the way a man treats them? I just didn't get it. My only conclusion was that I touched on a VERY sensitive topic.

I swear I'm not a man hater. Nor am I sexist. I am just me. My only objective was to help women by showing them how to beat men at their own game. So, men can play the game? But, the girls can't join in on the fun? I don't think so. The fact of the matter is that pussy power changes women into fierce, strong women that can't be taken advantage of. Apparently, there were some people that didn't like that.

Thankfully, I had powerful women to look up to and emulate. Women like Roseanne, Trina, Beyoncé, Madonna and countless others within my own personal life. These kind of women are brave, and they light the way for those of us still finding our way out of the dark. They're the type of women that won't bow down, that stir up controversy, break through boundaries, command respect, refuse to apologize, and create change.

These women reminded me that when you're a powerful and strong-minded woman, you're going to face some criticism. And as a woman implementing pussy power, you should remember that too. You're going to piss some people off. You're going to be criticized, labeled, and judged for going against the patriarchy's definition of how a woman should behave. Don't fall for it. Do not let society guilt you.

I have since come to accept that pussy power is a controversial topic that's going to get attacked no matter what I say. I can live with that. I would rather come under attack and face negative reviews than to keep this information bottled up. The patriarchy would like to keep pussy power swept under the rug, but it's too late! Pussy power will no longer be a secret. The cat's out of the bag and the dogs of the world will just have to learn to deal with it.

Sharing this information has empowered and strengthened thousands of women and that's what some people are truly afraid of. **Strong women only intimidate weak men.** There were lots of other men that told me the book was 100% truth. That it was knowledge they would share with their sisters, daughters, and other women they loved. Good men had nothing to fear. It was only the players, cheaters, user, abusers, and womanizers that needed to be worried. So, why all the fuss?

I honestly think it's because there are some weak minded men in this world. Men that subconsciously fear what might happen if this level of female empowerment went global. Fear of what would happen to "them" if all women suddenly stopped enabling bad behavior from men. When I say "them," I'm not referring to the good men. We like the good guys and we're not mad at you. We love, honor, and respect the good men. When I say "them," I'm referring to the bad men, the mediocre men, the losers, the users, the abusers, the dead beat dads, the assholes, and the cheaters.

It's these men that fear what will happen if we all collectively and suddenly reject the unbalanced levels of respect and demand better treatment. They fear what will happen if from now on only good, quality men were to be treated with respect and rewarded with love. The mediocre men of the world would be forced to step up.

The balance of power has tipped in their favor for centuries. They don't want the scales evening out. Even worse, they don't want the scales tipping in our favor. Which is exactly what will happen when every woman on the planet understands, acknowledges, and utilizes her power.

We honestly could take over the world if we really put our minds to it.

That's why pussy power has been kept from us. That's why they get mad when we rebel against the control. That's why when we go against it, they use degrading words such as slut, whore, and feminist. They put a negative spin on it, so that we feel wrong or shamed when standing up for ourselves. They're going to try their hardest to keep things the way they are, and even after female liberation they've been successful at controlling the reins.

But why should we care? So what if we don't control the

reins or run the world? We live in a society that's run by men, big deal. Well, it probably wouldn't be such a big deal except that it's full of bullshit, hypocrisy, mind games, and double standards. What's good for the goose is not always good for the gander.

Patriarchy:
Bullshit, Hypocrisy, and Mind Games

You probably see and feel patriarchy happening in your everyday life but have become numb to its slimy tentacles reaching up your skirt. Half of the time we don't even notice it. That's because it's a normal part of our everyday lives. It presents itself in your career through sexual harassment and sexual bias. It may even present itself in your personal life through bad relationships, cheating, and/or abuse. It can even present itself in a simple setting, such as when you go for a jog in a pair of shorts on a hot summer day.

If you've ever felt frustrated, exhausted, confused, scared, disgusted, or angry with men in general, then you my friend have been victimized by the patriarchy. Once it's laid out in black and white on these next few pages, you will start to see that you're not crazy for feeling this way and you're not alone. Shit's fucked up. The patriarchy is happening to each and every one of us on a daily basis. We are bombarded with it, so much that we've become accustomed to it. We've unknowingly accepted the patriarchy's bullshit as normal.

Over the next few pages I'm going to give you some examples, and some of these examples I'm going to go into detail about. (Please note: I'm speaking in general. I'm not saying that all men do these things.) But for example, why is it that some men expect their wives to maintain a thin, slim figure throughout life, even after having children, but these same men think it's okay for them to have beer bellies and tits? There are actually men in this world that *expect* their wives to stay skinny, but feel that it's okay for them to be overweight. Have you ever in your life seen a fat woman telling her sexy, muscular husband that he needs to get to the gym or that he shouldn't be eating that fatty food? I'm pretty sure the answer's no.

Think about this for a moment. Why is there no birth control for men? We have 12 options, most of which have serious side effects such as stroke and death, but not one single option for men, besides condoms? They're the main ones that want to stick it in, but *we* have to live with the side effects? Oh and while we're on the subject... where's our Viagra? Hypocrisy.

For an example of the bullshit, let's use sexual harassment. As women, we get sexually harassed **all the time.** I don't think the good men of this world realize how much we're bombarded with unwanted sexual advances. There are penises everywhere and they're constantly being offered to us. It really gets annoying. Especially because it always seems to come from old, perverted, gross men that we have no interest in.

It happens at work, school, and in the streets. It especially happens when we're young and naive to the fact that it's even happening. It's unfortunate, but I can guarantee that a majority of women reading this book can recollect at least one time in their life when they were sexually harassed.

When I was 16 years old, my driver's ed. coach was a big pervert. He flirted with all the girls. He encouraged us to wear tight pants to class in exchange for a pass on the driver's ed. test. What sixteen year old girl isn't dying to get her license? So, we all stupidly wore our tight pants and in the end, we got our driver's licenses.

The fucked up part is that we all passed our tests and we were more than deserving of our licenses with or without the help from our tight pants. It wasn't even about us wanting a free pass as much as it was about us being fearful that he might fail us if we didn't oblige. He used his position of power not to be a role-model and an educator, but to be a pervert.

I look back now and think how disgusting that was of that old man and how I should have denied his advances and turned him in to school authorities. However, as I mentioned earlier, when you're young and naive, you laugh these things off. The only thing you can think to do in the heat of the moment is to try and get out of the situation as peacefully and quickly as you can.

Another time was when I waited tables. The manager was such a pervert. He was constantly making sexual advances at us. Every girl that worked in that restaurant was a victim of his harassment. But again, we liked our jobs, and so we all just ignored it and swept it under the rug.

In both situations, I was uncomfortable at the time it was happening. However, I was so young and naive that I didn't really know how to handle the situation, so I usually laughed it off in an attempt to escape the situation. It's not until now that I'm older, I can look back upon my youth and think, "Damn, that was fucked up of those men. They were taking advantage of their positions of power and trust. They were using their twisted wisdom of knowing that I was young and naive."

I'm not claiming that every man that makes sexual advances is a harassing pervert. It's just that there's a time, a place, and a way for making sexual advancements. Making young women feel uncomfortable with continual uninvited advances is not necessary and it's very annoying. Doing it from a position of power and using that position to get away with it is simply disgraceful and unfair.

I could keep going with stories of all the times I was harassed. It happened time and time again over my young years. In fact, it happened so much that I remember a feeling of relief when I gained weight, because finally the perverts of the world had no interest in me. That's how much we're bombarded with unwanted sexual advances. Unfortunately for us, walking around with a healthy figure is an automatic invitation for unwanted perversion.

I honestly don't think men realize how much this goes on in our day to day lives. I don't even think we realize it when it's happening. We just know that it makes us uncomfortable, but we're so used to it happening that we've become accustomed to it. It's not until we're older and wiser that we come to realize what happened was actually sexual harassment. Unfortunately, by then it's too late to do anything meaningful about it, and who knows if anyone would have even listened anyway.

Unfortunately, our own naivete allows this behavior to continue and generation after generation of women and girls are subjected to it. That's one of the reasons why they do it to younger girls and they do it when they're in positions of power. They know we're vulnerable. They know that we won't want to stir up controversy, lose our jobs, or get anyone into trouble. Therefore, it remains a secret part of our society that's rarely discussed and simply swept under the rug.

The Evil Side of Patriarchy

Some of us aren't so lucky to simply be harassed. Some of us are molested and raped. Recently a news story of a teenage girl being raped and molested by four of her male "friends" has made headlines. The story blew up in the news because she's being criticized for ruining the young boys' bright futures as football stars. She's also being accused of lying. What's wrong with a society that denies accusations of rape in favor of saving a boy's promising football career?

The father of one of the boys was on television claiming it was her fault for being alone with four boys and drinking. That's right. I forgot, rape is okay as long as she was drunk and surrounded by men at the time of drinking. That's when it's the girl's fault, because she was obviously asking for it. Simply existing in a room with four boys is an obvious excuse for them to rape her, and getting too drunk and passing out, well that's just a straight-forward invitation.

If that's how they excuse it, then let's turn that around on men. The next time a young man is in a room alone with four other girls, and they drink too much and he passes out, should it be excusable for them to rape him in his ass with a broom stick? When you turn it around on them, it doesn't sound as passive as before when it was a woman involved.

Do we, as a society, not respect our women enough to defend them from sexual abuse? Is it *that* hard to believe that four teenage boys would take advantage of a teenage girl who drank too much and passed out? Is it easier for us to believe that she was there because she wanted to have sex with four boys and then intentionally ruin their lives by reporting it as rape to the police? Does anyone really believe that she purposely wanted to destroy her own life and be embarrassed in front of her entire community? Where is the logic in that?

It boggles my mind the way we react to these types of stories. We've all been a little too drunk and/or been in situations where we shouldn't have been, but that doesn't give anyone the right to take advantage of us. Nevertheless, we get the blame. Her skirt was too short. She drank too much. She was flirting. Excuses, excuses. If a woman is passed out, lying naked on the floor, it STILL does not give anyone the right to touch her, let alone rape her. Yet in our patriarchal society someone, somewhere would defend the rapist and blame the woman.

What society fails to understand about these situations is that sometimes when we're young women, we can be really naïve. We're too trusting. We fail to realize how perverted guys can really be and so we assume they would never do something like that. Then we get ourselves into bad situations by being too nice, too trusting, and too naïve. By the time everything is said and done, we feel stupid and guilty. We feel like it's our fault. Which only perpetuates the problem. That's why a lot of females don't come forward when stuff like this happens. We blame ourselves.

This story hit close to my heart and I think that's why I get so offended when I hear stories like this. A similar situation happened to me when I was in high school. I want to share my story so that people have more of an understanding of how these things can and do happen and why. When I was 15, I was almost raped by 5 guys. Thank God, I can say "almost" because it was a very close call. Luckily, I escaped. However, I never told anyone about it, not even my mom, because I felt like it was my fault.

I was skipping school. On the way to the city bus stop, I ran into a group of guys. One of the guys I knew. We had met at an all-ages club and we'd been talking on the phone for about two weeks. I liked him and so when he invited me to go smoke a blunt with them, I foolishly agreed.

We all walked to a house that belonged to one of the guys. Inside the house we all smoked a blunt, talked, and hung out. Everything was fine. The guy I liked led me to the bedroom. I liked him and so I went with him, not thinking anything of it. We kissed and some light touching took place. Nothing too crazy or sexual, just a typical teenage make out session. While we were in the room, I noticed some loud banging that sounded like they were hammering. I paid it no mind and assumed they were fixing something.

After kissing and talking, things got a little heavy and that's when he pulled out a condom. I was not interested in having sex with him and I told him that I was not ready for that. He continued to pressure me and as I was denying his requests, I saw one of the other guys peeking into the room. That's when I got an eerie feeling. I got up, left the room, and went back into the living room. That's when shit got real.

I immediately saw that they had taken a piece of wood and nailed it over the front door. I was trapped inside the house with five guys surrounding me. I started to panic. I asked them what was going on. That's when they proceeded to tell me that I knew what I came there for and to stop playing stupid. They turned it around on me and made me feel so idiotic for being so naïve.

One of the guys seemed to be the leader of the pack and he was getting really mean about it. Almost as if he enjoyed torturing me with fear. The more I began to cry, the louder he would get. He yelled at me, "You don't go into a house with five guys and think you're not here to have sex." I was terrified.

I knew I was about to get raped by a gang of teenage boys. All I could think to do was to cry and apologize. I looked over to the boy that brought me there and with tears in my eyes, I looked at him with an expression of sadness and desperation. My tears must have gotten to him, because he went to the one boy guarding the door and asked to be let out. The door guard pulled out some nails and opened the door, and when the guy went out the door, I bolted out of there. I ran to the bus stop and went home.

For years, I never told anyone. I felt like it was <u>my fault</u>. I know if I had been raped by them, I probably still wouldn't have told anyone. Again, I would've felt like it was my fault. My fault for being so stupid. My fault for skipping school. My fault for being where I shouldn't have been, with people I shouldn't have been with. God only knows what kind of trauma I escaped that day. I'm very thankful that I wasn't raped and that the boy I liked had enough of a conscience to help me escape.

But what about the girls that *are* raped? I wonder how many of them keep it to themselves. Can we blame them? The ones that are brave enough to come forward take the chance of being blamed and shamed in front an entire community. There isn't a single other crime in the world that blames the victim. Rape is the only one.

Being a girl isn't easy. Being a girl that's sexually abused, or even worse, sexually abused and then blamed and ridiculed for it, is painful, traumatic, and damaging. It can be difficult to recover from.Sexual assault changes who a woman is. Thoughts and memories float around in her head, haunting her for years. She's no longer trusting of men. She's no longer able to live her life in peace because she's distrustful. Her perception of the world has changed forever. It leaves a permanent scar on her soul.

All of that pain and suffering just for one man to get five seconds of pleasure. And is it even for the pleasure of sex, or is it a sick and twisted pleasure of power and control that they're enjoying? Rape is so wrong on so many levels. The fact that women get raped on a daily basis and the way we treat the women who have been raped are two of the worst examples of the power of the patriarchy.

Rape, molestation, and sexual harassment are forms of abuse that take place every day in the lives of women. It may not happen to every woman... but it does happen every day. It happens a lot more than we care to admit or acknowledge.

If you're a young woman and these kinds of situations are happening to you, please know that you're not alone. You're not alone in feeling like it's your fault. You're not alone in feeling like you shouldn't tell anyone. You're not alone in being taken advantage of simply because you're a female. It happens to a lot of us.

Don't be afraid to stand up for yourself, because if a man is making unwanted sexual advances at you, molesting you, or raping you... it is wrong. It's not your fault. It doesn't matter if you were drunk, high, in a bad situation, or with people you shouldn't have been with. I know it's scary and uncomfortable to face the situation head on. It's scary to stir up trouble. But know that if a man's doing that to you, he's probably doing it to other women, and has probably done it in the past too.

I think some men defend other men in these situations, not because they're purposely trying to be mean or cruel, but for two reasons. One, they feel a tremendous amount of pressure from their peers not to tell or to get involved. (This is one example of how the patriarchy affects men). Secondly, they don't understand what it's like to be a girl. They just don't get it.

They don't know what it's like to be constantly looked at up and down, to feel like a piece of meat in front of wolves, or even worse to be shunned because you're not a sexy enough piece of meat. They have no idea how confusing it is to be told repeatedly by a male driven society to be sexy, perfect, and promiscuous; just not *too* sexy or promiscuous. We're confused. We have low self-esteem. We want attention. Unfortunately, a lot us look for clarity, acceptance, and attention in all the wrong places.

A lot of the time it's this longing for acceptance, love, and attention that tricks us into making foolish decisions. It leads us into thinking that a man's desire to have sex is an indication that he likes us. In situations where it turns out that's not the case, we're discarded and left feeling used.

We all live and learn before we wise up and escape the bullshit. However, it's my hope that both of these books will prevent a lot of this trial by error. It's my goal to provide young women with wisdom, self-esteem, guidance, and the means to handle all of the tough situations that we're all faced with when going through our adolescence and well into our adult lives.

Getting pressured into having sex under false pretenses, facing constant unwanted sexual advances, being raped and then getting the blame for it; these are all characteristics of our patriarchy. The power of the patriarchy excuses, ignores, and in some cases even encourages bad behavior from men. And at its worst, it puts the blame on women when it doesn't want to face the demons it has created.

And what about the music? You can have 1,000 songs that sing about getting laid, getting a woman into bed, or getting a woman to give it up. However, if a woman was to put out a song encouraging women to use men for money, or a song that said, "I don't want you, I just want you to fix my car", she would be vilified! She would immediately be labeled a selfish user, a money-hungry whore, or some other bashing statement.

So, even in our society's art, we're subjected to sexual advances and it's normal to us. Like I said earlier, we're numb to it. I saw a young man wearing a shirt the other day that said, "Cool story, Babe. Now go make me a sandwich." Ummm, no. Go jack your dick with your sandwich, you little fucker. What's wrong with this picture? Is our society so fucked up that guys wear this type of crap and think it's funny?

I'm going to make a shirt. It's going to say, "Cool story, Babe. Now go fix the toilet." Could you imagine? Men would hate it if we treated them with one ounce of their same shit. They would flip the fuck out!

Conditioning AKA MANipulation

It appears that things got twisted around to mainly benefit the males. And, I don't for one second think that MANipulation was an accident. Society is run by the males, so society basically conditioned the women to act and behave in ways that benefit the men.

To avoid scrutiny, we went along with it. How did this happen? Very easily, right in front of our eyes! The men collectively decided and stood up for "what's right," then they all defended each other and put down any woman (or man) who went against it.

For example, on Amazon there are a ton of books about "How to Get Women to Sleep With You." If you look at any of these book's reviews, they only have a few one star reviews from people being against the subject matter. However, if you look at a book like mine that speaks about female empowerment, whether it's a fun dating advice book or a serious intellectual book about women's rights, you will find a vast number of one star reviews from both men *and* women speaking out against the topics.

The men have collectively decided what's right and what's wrong and they've conditioned us to abide by the rules. When a woman goes outside the patriarchal box, she is ridiculed and called crazy, sexist, feminist, trash, slut, and a ton of other negative labels. Simply put, we get bullied for going against the grain and speaking out against what is considered "normal."

It's only been in the last few decades, mainly in the 60's with female liberation, that women began to wake up to the bullshit and started to reject it. Since then, a lot of us have come together and decided that we're no longer going to be coddled, told to sit down and look pretty, starve ourselves into physical perfection, and be discriminated against simply because we're women.

Things have been changing and will continue to change for the better. This change has been allowed to unfold because **we have collectively decided** that we're not going to allow ourselves to be put down or taken advantage of. We stood up for ourselves, and things have changed in a dramatic and awesome way. I'm proud of the accomplishments we've made. I'm grateful to the women before me that stood up for us and went against the norm. They faced a lot of adversity to get us where we are today.

However, we all can sense and feel that there's still a ways to go. It amazes me that the Lilly Ledbetter Fair Pay Act was only signed into law in 2009. It's now illegal to pay a man more than a woman for the same job. That's great news. But wait... 2009!!!??? This should have been illegal from the beginning of time! Actually, it should have never been an issue to begin with. It's moral and ethical code.

Everyday examples of gender discrimination like that one

are just a few of the things that make me scratch my head and say, "What the fuck is going on here?!" What's even more confusing is that some of the discrimination comes from women! Women who have been raised to think and act in the best interests of men. They've been conditioned to believe that this is feminism and feminism is a big no-no. They don't even realize how crazy they sound when they basically go against themselves. They're at war with their own vagina.

The negative tone associated with the word feminism is just another form of conditioning and MANipulation. It's become a word used by some men in a derogatory way to make women feel that defending their rights is wrong. Did you know that the word feminism doesn't actually have a single negative intention associated with it? The definition simply states "advocating the rights of women to be equal to those of men." What's so negative about that?

They're using MANipulation to make us feel bad for standing up for ourselves. Now that the negativity of that word isn't as effective as it used to be, they've changed the word to 'femi-Nazi'. Because we all know that standing up for one's self and speaking out against injustice is equivalent to murdering millions of innocent people?!?!

Do you know why there's so much backlash over such simple arguments? Why there's such hatred thrown at women who are defending the rights of other women? Because as I mentioned earlier, they don't want women figuring this stuff out. They don't want women to realize their power. **We are so powerful that they feel the need to put a lid on our power.**

They know, without a doubt, that if every woman in the world knew her worth, the world would be a different place. Women would run the world. They don't like the thought of that, so they figure it's just best if they keep us in the kitchen.

Woman's Work:
Drudgery and Dependency

Another way the patriarchy is able to get away with a lot of crap is by enabling dependency. They've somehow used their little mind games to trick us into believing that staying home and tending to the house, while the man works, is the almighty mecca of womanhood. We fell for it so hard that a lot of us still believe that we should be happy and grateful to stay home, cook, clean, and take care of our man.

I'm a stay at home mom. My point is not against being a stay at home mom. It's great. Don't get me wrong. Especially if you have a supportive partner and you enjoy doing it. However, there are issues with this subject that are rarely discussed. The problem is two-fold. On one hand we can easily fall into a trap of dependency. On the other hand, we get fucked over on bearing the majority of the work load.

First let's talk about the controversial subject of woman's work. We're made to feel like we get a great deal out of this arrangement, but we don't. "Woman's work" as they like to call it, is not as easy they think it is. Of course, men will argue till their heads fall off that it's simple and easy. Some may claim we're just complaining or we're lazy if we can't handle it. However, get any one of those men to do it for a week and they will all gain a deeper understanding and respect for how hard it truly is.

So, who convinced us that this was the grand achievement we should all be trying to attain? It's not simple, nor is it easy. It's drudgery. The work is never done. The cooking and cleaning never ends.

I mean how many times do I have to wash, fold, and put away loads of laundry before it's considered spousal abuse? How many years do I have to wash dishes, day in and day out, before I get to retire? How many times do I have to hear the question

"What's for dinner?" before I explode!

On top of the never-ending work load, there are no sick days, paid personal days, or lunch breaks. It's not a 40 hour a week job. It's a never-ending, over-worked, under-paid, exhausting, under-appreciated JOB. The only thing that makes it all worth it is being able to stay home and spend time with your kids. They wonder why women fought so hard to enter the workplace? It's easier to go to work!

Eventually, the women wised up and said to hell with this housewife, woman's work, slavery nonsense. Slowly things began to change but only after great resistance. Why so much resistance? I will tell you why. Dependency. A woman who depends on a man for all of her needs is put into a very tight spot. This tight spot can easily lead to abuse if placed into the wrong hands.

If a woman begins her young life by getting married, having kids, and becoming a housewife she has a good chance of missing out on opportunities for education and/or work experience. This leaves her completely dependent on her man for her needs and the needs of her children. What happens if her man begins to hit her or cheats on her? She gets stuck in a bad situation that she can't easily escape. This can enable an abusive man to get away with a lot of bad behavior, should he choose to use his woman's dependency to his advantage.

Now please, don't get me wrong. Many families have the dynamic of the stay at home mom and the working father and things work out beautifully and everyone lives happily ever after. I'm not saying every situation where the man works and the woman stays home is a bad situation riddled with abuse. I'm only pointing out the fact that when this dependency is used for evil, it can wreak havoc in the lives of women, and we need to be cautious and aware of it. Never get caught up in the patriarchal trap of dependency. Always be a woman with a backup plan.

How Patriarchy Affects Men

As I mentioned previously, the power of the patriarchy doesn't just affect women. It affects men as well. It encourages men to play roles that some of them may not be comfortable playing. Of course, there are men that are perfectly comfortable in their role of the macho, manly-man. That's great for them, but what about the men that aren't?

What about the men that are made to feel weak, uncomfortable in their own skin, or like lesser than a man simply because they don't fit perfectly into the patriarchal mold of what a man should be? Not only are these men made to feel inferior, but the lack of desire and respect from women can be damaging to their self-worth.

It's the same way the patriarchy makes us feel shamed or inferior when we can't live up to the physical perfection it's defined for us. Or, if we go too far with it, we're disrespected. The same thing is happening to the men, just in a different way.

So, what we end up with is a bunch of scared, confused, and damaged human beings. Good guys afraid to be good, sweet, caring gentlemen and bad guys being rewarded for being assholes. Good girls repeatedly hurt for being too trusting or nurturing and then turning into bitches as a defense mechanism. It's become a vicious cycle and everyone is unknowingly taking part in the insanity.

Nice Guys Shouldn't Finish Last

The only way to break the cycle is to start with us. We can't sit around and wait for the men to change. We've got to change. When we change, the men will follow our lead. They will follow our lead because we will collectively decide and stand by what is right. We will make them feel bad for not abiding by our rules.

One of the first things we need to implement and collectively follow is the fact that nice guys shouldn't finish last. Start fucking good guys and stop fucking the bad guys. This will lead to the greatest and most beneficial change for women, men, and future generations. ***Nice guys should be rewarded and honored for being gentlemen***.

You know honestly, there's some great men out there. We just refuse to give them the time of day. We foolishly fall into the trap of wanting to fuck the bad boy and then trying to make the bad boy settle down. When he shows no interest, strings us along, or cheats on us we get all sad and depressed. But, it's our own fault for falling for the patriarchy's bullshit.

Womanizers should not be considered sexy. They should be looked down upon with disgust. We don't really want to be a man's sexual conquest. We don't really want to tame the bad boy. What we really want are men that have ambition, men that provide, protect, and remain loyal.

We're turned on by the wrong things. Rather than becoming stimulated by a man that has a career, an education, ambition, integrity, and the desire to remain loyal we're worried about the assholes. You know, the guys with nice cars, cocky attitudes, no job, no ambition, or no desire to commit. Instead of desiring men that are kind and gentle, we desire the men that reject us, treat us like shit, or refuse to commit. That's why recognizing the power that rejection has over us is so important.

We've got to stop settling for less and start expecting more from men. We've got to start rewarding the good men and punishing the bad ones by being smart about who we're lying down with. Men are motivated by sex, and the fact that they've been able to easily get sex from us without having to work for it has made them lazy and unappreciative.

They don't have to commit. They don't have to marry us. They don't have to work. They don't even have to be nice. We've taught them to be that way. We reward men that treat us like shit. They see this, and so they give us what we want. So, it's our fault men act like assholes.

We're the only ones that have the driving force to make them change. It starts and ends with us. If we all collectively agreed to only fuck the nice guys, we would be amazed at how quickly men would change!

Also, I want to add that you should never believe the myth that there aren't any good men left. They're out there, but if you fall into the trap of believing all men are the same, or all men are dogs, you might not be open minded enough to recognize a good one when he comes around.

It's because of good men like my husband and countless others out there that I have faith in my daughters' futures. I have faith in men. I have faith that things have changed just enough that over the course of a few more generations we won't have too much hypocrisy, bullshit, and mind-games to deal with. We will kick the MANipulation to the curb.

We won't have to fight for common sense laws like the Fair Pay Act. We won't have women conditioned to go against themselves by going against women's rights. More importantly, we won't have to be called names like femi-Nazi, slut, or man-hater for speaking out against injustices.

Maybe we can get a break from damaging our bodies with birth control and let the men bear the responsibility for once. Maybe we can even get some Viagra! We will simply be able to live and let live with peace, harmony, and respect between both sexes.

When I mentioned earlier that women could rule the world, I want to be clear and honest, that's not really my aim. Fighting the patriarchy isn't about world domination. It's about creating a world of respect, fairness, equality, and more importantly BALANCE.

Too much of anything is a bad thing. Too much male or female dominance will create an unbalanced society. What we all need to focus on is continuing to work towards equality until there's peace and harmony for everyone. That's when the world will come together and heal.

Even if things remained the same until the end of time, the joke's on them. Women really do run the world. We do now, and we did in the past. We just do it behind closed doors. We're so smart that we do it without them even realizing it.

Behind every great and powerful man stands his great and powerful wife. Pussy power had its place in time throughout history, from women in powerful positions such as Nancy Reagan, Princess Diana, and Eleanor Roosevelt to Queen Nefertiti, Cleopatra, and Helen of the Trojan War. Even Hitler was under the spell of pussy power. Mwahahahaha...

Conclusion

Whether you're single, married, or divorced... you have the power. You are a woman, and that within itself is enough to make you powerful, but only if you let it. Unfortunately, the reality is that not every woman will use her power. For these women, they will never experience the joys of using feminine power to create the life they desire. This isn't about financial gain or any other superficial non-sense. This is about discovering true and lasting happiness by using your unique power to find an awesome man. It's about intentionally creating a life that's going to bless you with all that you deserve and desire.

It's about recognizing that you never have to tolerate cheating, disrespect, or bad treatment. You have the ability to move past anything a man throws your way, but only if you choose to. It's about realizing that you can easily find tons of other men willing to give you the love and respect you deserve. You never have to settle or squander your power on losers, users, abusers, and unworthy men.

So, if that means that you've got to utilize the power of staying single for a tiny bit longer than you would like, just know that when it's all said and done, you will be with a wonderful man that treats you like a queen. It may also mean that if you're married to a jerk that's never going to change, then you may have to be brave enough to transition into divorce. That's why there's even power in divorce.

The power of the pussy is an endless supply of fun, wisdom, sexuality, mystique, seduction, persuasion, joy, and confidence. It can bring true happiness into your life when used for your highest good. But, it's up to you to allow it to work in your life. Allow it to shine through your unique personality, through the confidence you exude, and through the type of treatment you expect from men.

Bring out your inner goddess in your own unique way and if you feel it's not working, then the problem usually has to do with who you're using it on. See, every man can be hypnotized by the power of the pussy, but not every woman can hypnotize every man. However, every man will fall under the spell of at least one woman in his lifetime. I don't care if he's the biggest player on the planet, there's at least one woman out there that has power over him.

So, if you're trying to use your pussy power on a man, and it's just not working, then you're just wasting your time and efforts. It's like swimming upstream. You can put in a ton of work and effort, but you're never going to get anywhere. Why continue to waste your time? Recognize when it's not working and be strong and brave enough to control your emotions and move on. That's how you use it wisely. You go to the men that want and desire you, not the other way around. If you do this, you will always be powerful.

Someone once told me, "Go to the one that loves you; don't go to the one you love, and you will always be happy." For women, this advice should not be taken lightly. It's a man's natural instinct to chase, conquer, and claim his woman. For some reason we started being the ones to chase, conquer, and claim men. That's when things got out of balance.

Now the men are resisting. They're turned off by it. In turn, they're running around having a great time at our expense. They've been able to get the milk for free, while completely shunning the idea of ever buying the cow. But, we're the ones passing out the free milk! We're the ones running around desperately saying, "Please buy my cow?!?!"

This has enabled them to have all the power, and it's left us drained and confused. We've got to get back to the natural order of things. We've got to stop trying to convince men to commit. We've got to flip the game back around on them. To accomplish this we've got to be the ones that desire to remain single until a man proves he's worthy of our heart and our hand in marriage.

Also, by remaining confident at all times, and by recognizing and using pussy power.

It's the women of the world that utilize the powers that have good men in their lives. They're the ones that get what they want from men. Whatever it may be, whether it's the proposal, the marriage, the kids, the house, or simply the love and respect they deserve.

Pussy power is more than just sexual motivation. It's about not tolerating disrespect or bad behavior from men. Remember, if you choose to stay with a man that's playing games or you're not satisfied with the way things are going, then you're sacrificing your own happiness. At the end of the day, you'll have no one to blame but yourself if you're not happy. Don't tolerate crap from men and you will never be in a crappy relationship.

The less women in this world are willing to put up with shit, the less men will be able to get away with it. They will be forced to change, but it all starts with us. Each and every one of us has a responsibility to ourselves, each other, and the generations of women coming up behind us.

We've got to be there for one another, and stop the hate. We've got to stick together just like the men do. We've got to collectively decide what's right and what's wrong and put down any man that goes against it. We've got to stop rewarding the bad guys, and start honoring the good men. We've got to stop being superficial by putting looks and social status above quality and integrity when it comes to choosing who we lie down with.

When we can accomplish this... the world will change. When we stop stabbing one another in the back for some dick, and come together instead... the world will change. When we all stop tolerating disrespect, whether it's in our personal lives or through the bullshit, mind games, and hypocrisy of the patriarchy... the world will change. When we stop giving away our most precious asset, whether that's through sex or by giving a man the most precious gift of life... the world will change.

Ladies, if that's not the definition of pussy power, than I don't know what is! What an awesome gift we've been given! What better time than now to utilize this gift! It's been done in the past, and it can be done again. We're the daughters and granddaughters of generations of women that fought for equality and fair treatment. Women that changed the course of history.

We owe them more than just being a man's one night stand. We owe them more than just being a man's mistress or side chick. We owe them more than just being some guy's baby mama. We owe them more than being an unappreciated and mistreated wife.

Pussy power is a big deal.

A huge deal. And remember, this isn't about taking over the world and conquering men. This is about making the world a better place for all human beings. This will never be accomplished at the rate we're going now. War doesn't work. Violence doesn't work. Ignorance doesn't work. The patriarchy doesn't work.

The only thing we have yet to try is love and nurturing. And who better than the women of this world to provide it with what it so desperately needs? We should do this for ourselves, but more importantly for our daughters... just like the generations of the past did for us.

The only difference between then and now is that feminine energy is more powerful than ever. So, just imagine what we can accomplish. Let's heal society. Let's heal the world. Let's make history. Let's show them the true meaning of pussy power.

Frequently Asked Questions

Below are some of the most frequently asked questions that I have received from readers.

I've read both books, but I'm still having issues with my guy?

Here's the number one thing about pussy power that I think a lot of ladies are still having a hard time accepting. It doesn't work on every guy. **It only works on guys that like you and desire you.** So, you've got to understand that if you're in a relationship with a guy and *you* are the one that wants him badly and *you* are the one that's head over heels in love, and he doesn't feel the same way about you... then you are in a **powerless position**. If you're with a guy that treats you badly, doesn't love you or like you enough to be good to you, you're in a really tough spot. The only things you can do in these situations are...

#1) Get rid of him and move on to better men. Don't make the mistake again of being the pursuer. That's a man's position. When a woman is the one chasing and pushing for love, and the man isn't on the same page with that, majority of the time it will do more harm than good. He will become uninterested and push away. In this situation, you're fighting an uphill battle and you're taking a huge gamble with your time and emotions.

That's a gamble that might not pay off, so you're better off cutting your losses, walking away, and moving on to date other guys. You can't change a man that doesn't want to change. If he were head over heels in love, or very stimulated by you, you could get him to change. You could get him to do a lot of things, actually. So, remember when men want and desire to be with you and not the other way around... that's where the power lies.

#2) Stay with him, but accept that you're settling for less than what you deserve just to be with this guy and that's **YOUR CHOICE**. You have no one but yourself to blame if things continue down a bad path.

#3) Pull back. Some people simply want what they can't have. Back away from the relationship just enough to make him wonder what's on your mind. Act turned off from him, as if you're losing interest. Text less, call less, and no longer rush off to be with him at his every request.

Observe how he responds to this. If he doesn't care and allows the relationship to drift apart, then you know he simply doesn't care. There's nothing you can do about that, but at least you know the truth of the situation and you can move on.

However, if he begins to act concerned and wonders what's going on, then you know he's just the kind of guy that doesn't want to be smothered. He wants what he can't have and when you're too clingy, it's an automatic turn off. Refer back to book one and use PEAK, just say it, the power of confidence, and the power of keeping yourself busy. They're going to be your best assets in a situation like this.

I already gave it up! Have I surrendered my power? Can I turn things around?

Possibly. It's a gamble at this point. What you need to do now is use PEAK and PES as ways of turning things around. There's almost always an opportunity to use PEAK and PES to your advantage. Make him wait for sex for a little bit longer than usual. Tease him, flirt with him, but don't give it to him the next time he's expecting it.

More importantly, don't allow him to guilt you. Flip that guilt around and be confident. Then, the next time he's horny, mention what you desire from him in the sexy tone. (For example, "If we're going to continue doing this, I need more of a commitment from you.")

Basically, seduce him into giving you what you want. If he doesn't react the way you want, cut your losses and cut him off the pussy. It's a gamble, but it can work depending on where his head is at (no pun intended).

If he's interested in you as a person, it will work. If he's just using you for sex, he will drift away over time or try to keep you on his back burner for sex. Don't let that happen. Don't let him get in your pants if he won't give you what you want. Don't waste your feminine power on anything less than what you want and desire from a man.

Can you give me some more examples of how to use the Prince Charming Test?

Just about anything could be used in the test. Do you need some pictures hung on the wall? A hard to reach light bulb replaced? Perhaps, you forgot your cash and have nothing to eat for lunch. Do you need some clothes picked up from the dry cleaners? Maybe you need an escort to a business party. Do you need a ride home from work? Maybe you need a handy man to come to your rescue or your oil changed.

What're this guy's talents? Focus on things he's talented with. If he's a mechanic and he has a problem with helping you fix a minor repair on your car, that guy is not interested in you on a deep level.

Also be smart about it. For example, if you ask a man to hang pictures or fix things but he's clueless when it comes to that kind of stuff, figure out another way to test him. Find a way to test him that brings out his natural talents and gifts. Allow him an opportunity to show off for you. Never forget to be thankful or appreciative. For an added affect, you can compliment him and stroke his ego.

Any situation where you would want a boyfriend/husband to help you out would be an ideal tester. A good man will come to your rescue. A good man that has feelings for you will be happy and eager to lend a hand. You don't want to get involved with a man that isn't willing to help you out. That's a waste of pussy power. Move on to another man.

Don't have sex or get involved with men that won't offer to help you with these kinds of things. That's a sign that he's not feeling you the way you may be feeling him or he's just a lazy, self-centered asshole. He wants some pussy, but he can't change a damn light bulb? No, Honey. I don't think so. Stay away from that kind of man.

A man that likes you or has feelings for you will want to do these things. He will be happy and eager to help you because he wants to be *that guy*. He wants to be *your* Prince Charming. And he doesn't want to allow any other man the opportunity to grab that spot. And lastly, there's no need to get carried away with chores and commands. He's not your slave. Yet. Just kidding...

...or am I?

He was all into me, but now he's acting distant. What do I do?

Pull back from him a bit. People usually want what they can't have. If you show that you're too interested, it may turn him off. Remember, it's natural for men to pursue us. When we get into the habit of chasing them and pursuing them, it tilts things into an unnatural dynamic. At times, this can turn men off and accidentally push them away.

That's why it's beneficial to stay single, keep yourself busy, and have your own life. You want to be in a position of power, where men are chasing you down for commitment and pressing you to spend your time with them. Not the other way around. You were probably doing this in the beginning and that's when he was interested, but then once you started having feelings for him, he began to pull away and act distant. Go back to the way you acted when he was into you.

We've been together for a while and I want to get married. How do I get him to propose?

Use "Just Say It" (without being the one to propose, of course). Wait for a PEAK moment and speak up. Let him know that you desire to be married someday and you want a romantic proposal. Sometimes you have to speak your mind. A lot of the time it's not that a man won't marry you, it's that he just doesn't realize that's where your head is at. Especially if you're the type of girl that doesn't speak up and expects your man to just know these things.

You've got to understand that guys don't think like we do. Romantic proposals and weddings can be the last thing on their minds, but if he truly loves you, he will give you what you desire. You just have to let it be known that's what you deeply desire.

In the first book I told you how I met my husband. I'm going to take a quick moment to tell you how I got him to propose to me. In 2004, about six months after we had moved out on our own together, we got pregnant with our first daughter. Oops!

Actually, she was planned. I can't lie. We were two young people crazy in love, and we both had just gotten really good jobs. It was our first time making decent money. I guess in our whirlwind of hormones and good paychecks, we felt it was time to have a baby. However, I had let it be known that I didn't want to have a baby without being married. I mentioned how I always dreamed of a romantic and unique proposal. I used "Just Say It" and PEAK to my advantage... as I always do.

Within a few weeks of finding out I was pregnant we were at the mall and we passed by a jewelry store that was running a sale. He dragged me in, applied for credit, got approved, and told me to pick out my ring. (How romantic, I know.) But this is how these things happen sometimes. Besides, our money was pooled together, so he wouldn't have been able to buy a ring without me knowing.

So, we bought the ring together, but they kept it to size it. Fast forward a few weeks, and I just knew a proposal was coming, because the ring was ready. I just didn't know how, where, or when this proposal was coming.

One day on the way home from work, he drove past the apartment. When I asked where he was going, he said to get water and milk. Thinking nothing of it, we drove a bit farther. That's when I started to get suspicious.

We drove by several stores and we were now heading farther and farther away from the apartment. I knew something was up; I just didn't know what. Then, we pulled into the gas station where we met. He pulled right up to pump 6, the same pump where I was pumping gas the night we met. He got out of the car, opened my door, and asked me to step out. That's when he got down on one knee, professed his love, and asked me to marry him. Of course, I said yes and the rest is history.

You can get the romantic proposal and the wedding you want. You just have to be with a man that truly and deeply loves you and wants to see you happy. You also have to be willing to speak up. Let it be known what you need from your man. He can't read your mind. Of course, we would all like to believe that men know we desire a bed of rose petals, champagne on ice, and candles, but some of them just aren't wired to do that stuff. So, if you want that stuff or you desire a romantic proposal... just say it.

I want to get married, but the man I love is not interested in marriage. What do I do?

Why are you with a man that doesn't want to marry you? If you want to get married, you can't waste your time being with a man that's not on the same page. You should cut your losses, and move on. Date men with similar values.

I know, I know... you love **him** and want to be with **him**. You don't want to date other men. I get it. But, here's the problem with that. You put yourself into a bad position by staying with a man that refuses to marry you. What if you stay for years and years and he never marries you? That's the gamble you're taking.

Which is fine; it's your life. But if you lose the gamble, then you've done that to yourself by loving a man that refused to marry you. That's the price you're paying to be with him. You deserve to get married, if that's what you desire. You shouldn't have to sacrifice your wants and needs to appease a man. There's a few things you can do in this situation to try and turn things around:

Give him an ultimatum. Then set a personal deadline. Set a time frame that you're willing to wait for a proposal. It could be a few months or a few years, but don't tell him. See what he does with your ultimatum. Give him a chance to figure out what he's going to do.

Then, if your deadline comes and he still hasn't budged, give him one last warning. The warning should include a deadline that you do verbalize to him. For example, you could say, "If I'm not engaged by the time I'm thirty, it will really break my heart. I don't want to leave you, but I've waited a very long time. If you're not willing to propose to me by then, I will have to move on with my life." If he still refuses, then you only have two choices. You either get prepared to leave him or give up your dreams of an engagement and marriage.

If I were you, I wouldn't waste years of my life waiting for a man. If you want to get married, you deserve to be married. If he refuses, then talk to him. Try to find out why. Then tell him that if he really loved you he would give you that honor. He wouldn't allow you to go through life as a single woman.

If the ultimatum fails, leave him and see what happens. Give him a few months on his own to realize how much he needs you. Sometimes they don't realize what they've got until it's gone.

Here's a book I recommend for women in this situation. It's called, "How I Got Him to Marry Me: 50 True Stories," by Cherise Kelley. It's a cute book filled with different stories of how women got the proposals they were seeking. Some used ultimatums; others used pussy power in some form or another, and some got lucky. You may get some good ideas. You may read some stories that make you cringe, and you may laugh, or see your own situation within the pages. It's fun to see how other women got their reluctant men to propose.

I want to be a stay at home Mom. How do I get him on board with me?

I would say that the most important part of being able to be a stay at home mom is to be with a man that is truly in love with you. When a man is very much in love with you, he wants to make you happy. Then you can use PEAK on this man. Using PEAK on a man that's in love with you will always get you a lot of what you want.

That's what I did. I didn't settle down and commit until I knew that I had a man that loved me deeply. Then, when the time came to talk about having kids, I would use "Just Say It." I mentioned how awesome it would be to be a stay at home mom. So, when I became pregnant I asked him (in a PEAK moment and very sweetly) if he would fulfill my dream of being a stay at home mom.

We made a financial sacrifice for a few years and didn't have much extra money, but it was a sacrifice we made together. We both agreed it was the right thing for our family and it was worth it for me to be the one raising our girls while they were young.

When trying to get your man on board with the idea, discuss all of the positives. But the main thing that's going to sell a man on the idea is agreeing to be 50/50. If he works, provides the money, and takes on the stress of paying all of the bills, then guess what that means for you? The joy of cooking, cleaning, and doing 90% of everything for the kids. It's only fair.

So, perhaps that's the main thing to mention in favor of your case. As I mentioned earlier, being a stay at home mom isn't easy. It's not for everyone. You need to be sure that you're prepared to hold up your end of the bargain, and you also need to be sure that your man can do the same.

It's so hard to wait 60 days. Do I really need to wait that long?

You're free to do whatever you like. You just have to accept responsibility if things don't turn out the way you want. If he hits and runs, you will have no one to blame but yourself. Having sex quickly is not a requirement for love. Stop letting music, men, media, and your hormones fool you into thinking that you've got to rush into sex.

If you've ever watched Jersey Shore, there's a perfect example within that hit television show. You've seen 100 girls come and go throughout the series. They get picked up at clubs, go back to the house, and have sex on the same night that they met one of the guys. Then they have to do the walk of shame on their way out of the house, never to be seen or heard from again. Lovely.

Now, remember the two girls that had Vinny and Pauly love struck? These two girls did not go home with the guys. They did not have sex with them. Out of all the girls they smashed on the first night, it was the girls that DIDN'T rush into bed that had the guys buying flowers and taking them on dates. It's the two girls that made them wait that got their love and respect.

The other thing to remember is that the guys pursued these girls. The girls didn't pursue the guys. They met at clubs, the guys flirted, the girls flirted, but the guys asked for their numbers, and the guys put in the work of calling and asking them on dates. These girls had their own things going on, their own lives, so they weren't all caught up into pursuing the guys. The guys were actively pursuing them. Not the other way around.

So, yes, for your pussy power to be the most effective, you really need to wait. If you can't make it 60 days, then can you at least make it past a couple of weeks? Let the passion build. Let the desire swirl around in their minds for a little while. Allow them a chance to earn it. They want to earn it.
There's a thousand girls out there ready to give it up. Be the one girl that doesn't.

It's not only important to make them wait for the first time. It's important to keep their attention by making them work for it all the time. Your pussy is special. It's not there for a man's entertainment or to be used as something to keep him happy and content. It's not a damn pacifier. That's what boobs are for!

Drake said it best, "She makes me beg for it, before she gives it up, and I say the same thing every single time. Baby, you the best. The best I ever had." Making men wait builds anticipation. It makes it extra special once they finally do get it. It works for the first time, and it works indefinitely.

Of course, you don't have to make him wait for sixty days after the first time, but you need to build anticipation. You need to reward good behavior, and punish bad behavior. You can't do that if you're giving it to him at every turn, in every which way, and especially if you're giving it to him when he's being an ass. That's not making him work for it. That's spoiling him.

Here's another way of looking at it. You know how waiting, anticipating, and planning for a vacation is almost as fun as the actual vacation? If you went on vacation all the time, it wouldn't be as special or exciting. You would get used to it. Eventually you would yearn for bigger, better, and more extravagant vacations. You would get spoiled and the novelty would wear off.

So, making a man wait and earn your body is important for the above reasons, but there's several other important reasons. It builds respect. It lets you know where he stands as far as his true feelings for you, and it weeds out the men that are simply looking to use you for sex.

And by the way, if you're just looking for sex, then you have the right and freedom to fuck whoever you want, whenever you want. But, don't lie to yourself if you're really looking for love or a long term relationship. If that's what you truly desire, I will always suggest that you make him wait. Sixty days goes by in a flash. Have some patience. Let the desire build until it's boiling over. The day you finally let him have it, it will be the best he ever had.

He's checked out emotionally. Why do you think this is? What can I do about it?

Sometimes when we enter into new relationships everything starts off hot and heavy. Things were going great, and just when you really begin to dig a guy, he pulls the rug out from under you! Out of nowhere he seems to lose interest. It's almost as if the moment he knows for sure that you're interested in him is the moment he backs off, checks out emotionally, or disappears. Why do men do this? It's so frustrating!

I believe there are three reasons why this happens. The most common reason why is because men want what they can't have. They like the thrill of the hunt. He was all into it in the beginning, because he wasn't sure how you felt about him. Once he knew for sure he could have you, he lost interest. He checked out emotionally. If you think this may be the case with your guy, the best thing you can do is to beat him at his own game. Back off and see what happens.

You have to make him feel that he's losing his chance. The only way you can do this is to act uninterested. I'm not saying you should ignore him. You just need to pull back... a lot. If this is the reason for his emotional check out then he will slowly begin to step his game up. However, do not jump the first time he asks! Keep your "emotional distance" until you notice a lasting change in his behavior.

If the change is not the one you want, control your emotions and move on to the next man, because that's proof he wasn't into you (or he was, but lost interest). However, if he truly likes you, he will realize that he's losing the game again. In some cases, that will be enough to re-spark his interest.

Even if he does start to pursue you again, but you're kind of iffy about him since he pulled out the MANipulation tactics, then you can always have fun with him by playing mind games. Yes, I know, mind games are wrong. Whatever. Men toy with our emotions all the time and it's no big deal. Why do people have an issue with it when we do it?

You can play mind games by having one foot in the relationship and one foot out of the relationship. Flirt, but don't make any moves. Flirt, but don't give in to sex/sexual stuff. Flirt, but don't pursue a relationship. Send him mixed messages. String him along. Act aloof. Confuse him. Does she like me? Does she not?

The second reason why this emotional check out happens is when a man gets scared of commitment. He may see that the relationship is moving forward and turning into something serious. This scares some men. It scares them for different reasons.

One reason could stem from a fear of getting hurt. Another reason could be when they're still emotionally attached to an ex. If they still have feelings for an ex, they may not be ready to let go of the past. And probably the most frequent reason why is due to a fear of leaving behind the single life. Heaven forbid if he settles down with a great girl, the freedom of his single life will be lost forever! That's a reality some men are just too scared to face.

If you think your guy is just scared of commitment, and you feel like you can be open with him about these issues, then talk to him.

Use a session of PEAK and "Just Say It" to get to the bottom of things. And please, by all means, if he doesn't communicate with you in a way that satisfies your curiosity, don't have sex with him.

The third reason why this emotional shut down can happen is a reason that none of us want to hear. You may have done something that turned him off or you've been put on the back burner. Simple as that. If this is the case, there probably isn't much you can do about it other than try and trouble shoot his emotional check out by going through the first two suggestions above.

However, if both of the reasons and tips above do nothing to help the situation, then he may have simply lost interest for some reason. Or, you were a front burner chick when he found someone else and you got moved to the back burner. Either case sucks, and it can hurt really bad, but don't let rejection get to you. It happens to the best of us. Everyone gets the shaft at some point in their love life.

We Keep Bumping Heads. What Do I Do?

Sometimes a woman can enter into a relationship with a really awesome guy, but for some reason they keep bumping heads. It's my opinion that sometimes this can happen when the balance of power is off kilter. You see, no other dating advice book will ever say something like this, but it's my opinion that overall there's a leader and a follower in every relationship.

Whether it's the male or the female, someone is in the driver's seat. Someone is the pursuer, and someone is the pursued. Someone is the dominant person, calling the shots, while the other person is happy to be along for the ride. There's nothing wrong with this fact. It's really just a personality preference.

For example, perhaps you're more comfortable being the dominant one, but you've suppressed this natural side of your personality to be with your man. Or, it could be opposite, where you prefer to be more submissive, but you're with a man that's very laid back and likes to let someone else lead. Think about if this could be a reason for the tension in your new relationship. If it is, then this can frustrate you without you even realizing why.

This type of unbalance goes on all the time in relationships, unbeknownst to and unrecognized by the people involved. All they know is that there's tension and aggravation. If you're compromising a part of yourself, issues will arise. Especially when personality preference is ignored, or even worse, suppressed for the sake of pleasing or attaining the love of another person. You should analyze your preference and appreciate it. Don't deny an important part of who you are for the sake of another person. Denying an important part of your personality can cause an unbalance in the dynamic of your relationship.

Many people are going to have an issue with this subject. They may claim it's sexist or untrue. However, I think if you sit and really think about it, it's an undeniable fact within the world of relationships. There's always a more dominant person in the relationship and this person is usually the leader, the shot caller so to speak.

In the past it was generally the men that were the leaders of the relationships, but things have changed. Of course by society's standards, that's the natural order of things but fuck society's standards. I'm sure a lot of you have grandmothers and mothers that run the show. So, while society might like to believe that men are the dominant ones, a lot of the time it's the women taking the lead. Some women may even be kind enough to allow it to appear as the man is in control when behind closed doors, both partners know good and well that the woman is in charge.

It's really all about balance and finding what makes each person happy. It's about finding the yin to your yang. The salt to your pepper. **Finding this balance brings comfort, harmony, and peace to relationships.** If you're bumping heads with your new guy, sit and analyze if it could be due to either one of you denying a side of yourself.

Recognize which role you prefer to play and never deny it for a man. For example, you may be the kind of woman that needs to lead all the time and in every way. Well, then you're going to bump heads with a man that has those same needs. You need a man that doesn't mind sitting back, one that allows you to lead. Or, perhaps you're the type of woman that prefers the man taking the lead in all aspects of life. Then you're going to be very unhappy dating a man that's dependent or needy. You need a take charge kind of guy.

Really take the time to figure out who you are before you get stuck in some dynamic that doesn't work. This is important for your happiness. It eliminates frustration. When people can be honest about who they are and the roles they prefer to play, there will be no head bumping.

Song List

God Bless the Broken Road by Rascal Flats (Rejection is Redirection)

These Tears I Cry by Estelle

Take a Bow by Rihanna

Runaway by Kanye West

A Little Bit Stronger by Sara Evans

Since U Been Gone by Kelly Clarkson

Part of Me by Katy Perry

You Don't Own Me by Joan Jett

Strong Enough by Cher

Wrecking Ball by Miley Cyrus

Forget I Ever Knew You by Clay Aiken

These Boots Were Made For Walking by Nancy Sinatra

Done by The Band Perry

Alive Again by Cher

Don't Want You Back by Backstreet Boys

Grow A Pear by Ke$ha

Bye Bye Bye by NSync

Come N Go by Pitbull

Jar of Hearts by Christina Perry

Crooked Smile by J. Cole

Wasting All These Tears by Cassadee Pope

Lock My Door by Jeff Floyd

Titanium by David Guetta

You Haven't Seen the Last of Me by Cher

Bullet Proof by La Roux

Bitter by Chante Moore

It's a Metaphor, Fool by Say Anything

Bitch, I'm Special by Rihanna

Try Sleeping With a Broken Heart by Alicia Keys

Girl on Fire by Alicia Keys

Cater 2 U by Destiny's Child (The Power of Food, Sex, and Loyalty)

Body Party by Ciara (The Power of Food, Sex, and Loyalty)

Psalms 23 by India Arie

Printed in Great Britain
by Amazon